W9-BNT-926

101 Quick Tips For A Dynamite Resume

Books by Richard Fein

101 Quick Tips For a Dynamite Resume

101 Dynamite Questions to Ask At Your Job Interview

111 Dynamite Ways to Ace Your Job Interview

Cover Letters! Cover Letters! Cover Letters!

First Job

101 Quick Tips For A Dynamite Resume

Richard Fein

IMPACT PUBLICATIONS
Manassas Park, VA

Copyright © 1999 by Richard Fein

All rights reserved. Printed in the United States of America. No part of this book may be used or reproduced in any manner whatsoever without written permission of the publisher: IMPACT PUBLICATIONS, 9104-N Manassas Drive, Manassas Park, VA 20111, Tel. 703/361-7300.

Library of Congress Cataloguing-in-Publication Data

Fein, Richard
    101 quick tips for a dynamite resume / Richard Fein.
        p. cm.
    Includes bibliographical references and index.
    ISBN 1-57023-082-X (alk. paper)
    1. Resumes (Employment) I. Title.
HF5383.F364   1998
650.14—dc21   98-33533
                                                        CIP

For information on distribution or quantity discounts, telephone (703/361-7300), fax (703/335-9486), email (*info@impactpublications.com*), or write to: Sales Department, IMPACT PUBLICATIONS, 9104-N Manassas Drive, Manassas Park, VA 20111-5211. Distributed to the trade by National Book Network, 15200 NBN Way, Blue Ridge Summit, PA 17214, Tel. 1-800-462-6420.

Contents

v

Chapter 2: Getting Started 14

Chapter 3: Planning Before You Write 24

Chapter 4: Heading 30

Dedication

In Memory of my Aunt Dot

and

In Memory of my Uncle Harry

Acknowledgments

I would like to thank the following individuals, most of whom are human resource professionals, who either read portions of this book's manuscript and shared their comments with me or who shared insights about resume writing with me in other ways. Of course, any errors of content, opinion, or presentation remain strictly my own. Inclusion in this list does not imply endorsement of this book's contents.

Thomas L. Adkins	University of Cincinnati
Amy Andrzejewski	Aurora University
Linda J. Bayne	Gill/Balsano Consulting
Roseanne Bensley	New Mexico State University
Clint Berge	Arkwright Mutual Insurance Company
Patricia Bergmaier	Georgia Southern University
Natalie Brandon	Northwest State Community College
Sterling M. Brockwell, Jr	Moffatt & Nichol Engineers
Frank Brennan	BOC Gases
Deborah L. Brower	Aeroquip Corporation
Russell A. Bruch	California State University, Sacramento
Michael J.P. Burns	Hunter Douglas, Inc. - WFD
Laura Buscaglia	Chase Manhattan Bank
Lindsay Carter, Jr.	Bellsouth Telecommunications
Tom R. Cath	DePauw University

Nylah Chilton	AgAmerican, FCB/Western Farm Credit Bank
Michael Crouch	Reasoning, Inc.
Keely Czop	Lockheed Martin
Derek J. Dozer	The Longaberger Company
Dan J. Emmel	East Tennessee State University
Christopher F. Farrell	Keyence Corporation of America
Dee Giffin Flaherty	Carlow College
John Flato	Cigna Corporation
Albert J. Frazia	Insignia Financial Group
Jim Glossbrenner	Angelo State University
Betty J. Goyette	Agway, Inc.
Karin Hanson	Enterprise Rent-A-Car
Jane Halliwell	Convance
Jeannine A. Harrold	Bell State University
Gail Hafer	Algent Health
Gary S. Hunt	OMI, Inc.
Jill C. Jurgens	University of Cincinnati
Steve D. Kelly	G.A. Sullivan
Tom Kilpatrick	USS-POSCO Industries
Randy Kriby	Nations Credit
Jana Kolakowski	Schlumberger ATE
Joe Kozlarek	Purina Mills, Inc.
Sharon B. Kurtt	Institute of Technology, University of Minnesota
Jennifer Lab	The National Dispatch Center, Inc.
Monica Lond	Mount St. Mary's College
Lori Long	PHR
Nancy J. Manter	Kollsman, Inc.
Joseph E. Marosits	Cytec Industries
Carol L. Miller	OSF St. Joseph Medical Center
Linda Mundy	Southwest Gas Corporation
Mary J. Nissen	Ascent Solutions, Inc.
Mark S. Phillips	Exigent International
Michael Placencia	California Department of Water Resources
Michele Pomeroy	TTX Company
Paul R. Powers	Digital Equipment Corporation
Susan E. Race	CERAMCO
Bob Reynolds	Chadron State College
Adrienne Rosenfield	Moody's Investor Services
Theresa W. Stiefer	Cameron University
Edward M. Turose	The Institute for Motivational Living, Inc.

Introduction

A Book With 100 Contributors

This book reflects in part my eighteen years of experience as a career coach. However, I have been fortunate to receive input from dozens of other career professionals, most in corporate human resources, who read parts of the book's manuscript or who shared their thoughts with me in other ways. It is with sincere gratitude that I list their names in the Acknowledgments.

How This Book Will Help You

101 Quick Tips For a Dynamite Resume is designed to help you write a dynamite resume in five ways:

Easy to Start: Writing a resume can be a daunting task. This book provides you with some key principles and then a step-by-step unfolding of the resume process.

Easy to Follow: The 101 Tips are succinct, compact explanations which are easy to identify. There is no risk of getting lost in a running text.

Easy to Review: If you want to review something you have read, the Table of Contents will help you find the Tip you need in a flash.

Easy to Change: Many Tips show you a number of alternative approaches depending on your job search situation. That will help you modify your resume to address different job opportunities.

A De-Mystified Approach: Every Tip is explained clearly and in a down to earth manner. When you use this book to write your resume, you will realize that there is really nothing mysterious or frightening about writing a dynamite resume.

The Job Search Club

During the course of this book we will be referring to members of a hypothetical Job Search Club. Each member represents a person with a somewhat different job search situation. Throughout the book, we will be referring to one or more of these people in connection with resume issues of particular significance to them. You may find that one of the JSC members described below has a job search situation similar to yours.

Rhonda: A business professional moving up within her current profession.

David: An established professional seeking to change either the functional nature of his work or to move to another industry.

Gabrielle: A scientist looking for a new job.

Larry: A recent college graduate seeking his first professional level job.

Lauren: A person returning to the full-time work force after a ten year absence.

Some Important Words

Throughout this book, we will use a consistent vocabulary to make your reading that much easier. Each term will be defined when it is first used, but a short list at this point may be helpful.

Basic Parts of the Resume

Heading: Provides administratively important information about you, including your name, address and phone number(s). Usually the heading goes on the top of your resume, but this is not an absolute necessity.

Summary: A short statement indicating skills and attributes you possess which would be important for your next employer.

Experience: A section on your resume which indicates your positive characteristics, usually in the context of a job you have held. Experience could include volunteer positions and even class projects in some cases. Experience provides an opportunity to show that your past and present offer value to a future employer. Experience will always describe you in terms meaningful to your *next* employer. Only rarely will Experience be a list of job descriptions.

Education: At a minimum Education will show what degrees you have earned and your major field(s) of study. However, we will see that Education can tell much more about you than that.

Other Selling Points (OSPs): Strengths that you have which do not fit neatly as part of Experience or Education. Civic awards would be one example.

Other Terminology

Recruiters: In this book "recruiter" will be the person who reads your resume to determine whether or not you should be invited to an interview.

Positive Characteristics: Skills and attributes that you have demonstrated, achieved or learned which would be of value to your next employer.

Schema: We will use this term to indicate the main divisions of your resume without the accompanying text.

Text: The words you use to describe your positive characteristics or critical data in your Experience, Education or Other Selling Points.

One Page-Human Eyes

This book contains tips about scannable resumes, e-mail resumes and faxing so that you will have that information when you need it. We also provide examples of a two-page resume and reasons for utilizing it. However, most of our tips are presented in the context of a one-page, paper resume designed to be read by a human being. There are several reasons for doing this:

- For most people a one-page resume is the best approach.

- The basic principles of resume writing skill apply to a two-page resume as well.

- The preponderance of paper resumes are read by human beings at the selection stage, and not scanned by Optical Character Readers (OCRs).

- OCRs are becoming increasingly sophisticated. Most paper resumes are now scannable in any event.

- E-mail changes the mode of delivery and format of your resume, but it does not change its content.

- Even resumes which are retrieved from databases are read by a recruiter before a decision is made to invite the applicant to a job interview.

These important facts are drawn from responses to survey of 1,000 employers nationwide which I conducted in the summer of 1997.

If you would like to share your ideas about this book with me, I can be reached by e-mail at *rfein@som.umass.edu*

Richard Fein
June, 1998

1

General Principles

The tips in this chapter are general principles to keep in mind even before you start writing your resume.

TIP #1: What is a Resume?

Your resume presents the professional "you" on paper in a clear, brief, honest and reader friendly manner. It is an advertisement which says "It is in your interest as an employer to interview me because of what I can do for your company." A good resume will **increase the probability** of your being interviewed, which is often the hardest part of the job search process. However, even the best written resume provides no guarantee that you will be invited to an interview.

When possible, your resume should be focused on the specific job opportunity you are seeking. Therefore you may develop different resumes for different situations.

TIP #2: Your Resume is an Investment

The time you spend on your resume is an investment in your career. If you take writing your resume seriously, you can benefit in five ways.

➤ **Self analysis:** Since the subject of your resume is **you,** writing your resume well forces you to think about your professional self in a concerted way.

➤ **Inventory of your strengths and accomplishments:** One step you will take is developing an inventory of your strengths and accomplishments. Even those items which do not ultimately appear on your resume can be useful in writing a cover letter or as talking points at your job interviews.

➤ **Identifying weaknesses:** The characteristics you **cannot** honestly include on your resume are telling you something. First, you might try to find opportunities on your current job or elsewhere to demonstrate, achieve or learn the characteristic you are missing. Second, what you **don't say** on your resume may be perceived as a potential weakness if you are interviewed. At your interview, be prepared to discuss what's missing on your resume.

➤ **Influencing the interview agenda:** Your resume will often serve as a source of interview questions. Therefore, what you write helps to set the interview agenda.

➤ **Resume as interview preparation:** The effort you put into writing your resume also helps you prepare for interviews. After all, the resume shows a potential match between the job and your skills, which is the main topic of your interview.

TIP #3: Thirty Seconds?!—That's Plenty

If you follow my advice, you will invest many hours of work to write a resume which will win interviews. How long do you think the employer spends reading a resume, on average?

When I ask people this question, I usually get a range of answers from 10 seconds to two minutes. In fact the average time spent on reading a resume is closer to 30 seconds.

"Thirty seconds!! That's not very long" you might say. You'd be right. But it is a fact, so we have no choice but to live with it. In addition, it's a fact which flows from a good reason: If you have a message worth reading, 30 seconds is plenty of time to get it across. Just think of television commercials. If you don't have a good message, even a two-minute reading won't get you invited to the interview.

TIP #4: One to Reject; Two to Accept

Most resumes submitted will not result in a job interview. One reason is sheer volume. A second reason is resume quality. A true story will illustrate these points. A friend of mine—let's call him Jerry—was a recruiter at a large corporation. Jerry was designated to identify three candidates for a hiring manager's consideration. Ultimately, only one person was to be hired. In response to a newspaper ad, he received 200 resumes. My friend calculated what he would need to do. To find three second round candidates he would need to invite 12 people to an initial interview. Therefore 200 - 12 = 188 resumes **to be rejected.**

This is what my friend looked for:

- High profile matches. In the first review these went into a "maybe" pile

- Resumes lacking a quickly identified match or containing a knock out like poor organization, unprofessional appearance, misspelling or apparently inapplicable career goal, were quickly rejected.

To reach the "maybe" pile a resume needed to meet two key conditions:

1. a quickly identified match

2. no knock outs

To be rejected, a resume needed only to be on the wrong side of either condition.

The resumes in the "maybe" pile were reviewed by both my friend and the hiring manager to identify 12 for interviewing. This is not uncommon. It takes only one person to reject your resume, but it may take two to act on it favorably.

TIP #5: What to Assume About the Recruiter

The person who reads your resume might have many titles and/or responsibilities. For ease of presentation, we will use the terms "recruiter" in this book.

If you are going to form a mental picture about the recruiter, assume two things about him/her: Very intelligent; completely ignorant about you. Let's take a look at both parts.

- **Very Intelligent:** The person reading your resume is intelligent enough to have his/her job and will have some input about a job for you within that company. Assuming the best is both more accurate and more comforting than assuming the worst.

- **Completely Ignorant:** What the recruiter knows about you is only what you wrote on your resume. The "you" which is invited to an interview or sent a no interest letter is the "you" presented on your resume.

TIP #6: What Your Resume Isn't

A resume is not a curriculum vitae, your autobiography or your last will and testament.

A resume is a brief presentation of true statements which give clearly identifiable reasons to interview you. For most people, their resume should be one page. In certain professions, such as academia, a curriculum vitae (or "vita") may be requested. These tend to be much longer and include details such as conference papers delivered and publications. The curriculum vitae approach is a disaster except in the limited professions which call for it.

Many people become emotionally attached to their resume. Let's put things in perspective: You are not trying to tell the world who you are or to ensure that you will be remembered well by posterity. Stay focused on your much more limited but obtainable goal: To write an honest resume that will lead to job interviews.

TIP #7: Write Your Own Resume

Since writing a good resume can be difficult, some people try to find a short cut. That can be a big mistake.

- **Temptation by Template:** There are a number of computer CD's on the market intended to help write a resume. These CD's include a template which is designed to mold or pattern your resume. Unfortunately, following the template often induces people to write a resume which reads like a job description, and that is not to your advantage. Resume CD's may also provide a large number of resume sentences for your selective use. You could take a line from the CD here, a thought from there, fill a page and call it a resume. But a resume developed this way is not likely to describe **you** or hold together as a coherent presentation. You would also lose the important benefits of insight and interview preparation which flow from preparing a resume from scratch. If you utilize a resume CD at all, use it to generate ideas and not as your main approach to writing your resume.

If you are responding to an employer's Web site or an electronic database, templates may have a different role (see Chapter 11).

- **Professional resume writer:** There are properly trained people who can help you identify your strengths and match them with an employer's needs. Don't take a potentially good thing too far, however. Never have another individual simply write a resume for you. You will gain nothing from the resume development process. What's more, if a resume looks like **you** didn't write it, you are less likely to be invited to interview. "If you didn't write, I won't invite" might be a recruiter's slogan.

TIP #8: Your Goal Is to Be a Good Match, Not Simply to Be Different

A common notion people have when writing a resume is that they want to "stand out." However, there are two distinct approaches to doing that. The positive approach is to show that you are a **good match** for the prospective employer's needs. This would truly make you stand out: Most applicants do not show on their resume a plausible match with the position they are seeking, even when they actually have the skills and attributes needed.

The negative approach is simply to stand out by being different. Writing a resume which is eye-catching but without the appropriate substance is not likely to win an interview. As an extreme example, cut your resume in the shape of a paper doll. Stand out? Yes. Will it lead to an interview? Probably not.

TIP #9: Don't Update Your Resume—Rewrite It

Many of the people I counsel think they can simply update their existing resume. "My current resume helped me get this job," Rhonda, an experienced marketing professional, exclaimed. "I will just add-in the new things, and I am set." Larry, a college senior, had a similar thought. "I'll just add in my summer job and my part-time job this semester," he said.

"You could do that and not get arrested," I responded. "But that won't help you produce your strongest possible resume." Here's why:

If you simply put a new experience on top of your old ones, your resume is likely to become long, repetitive and unfocused. The best approach is to start from scratch. Then refer to your existing resume to see if you have left out something which should be included. As a second best approach, review your existing resume with the idea that it might need to be revised significantly.

TIP #10: Write In "Resume-ese": The Art of the Telegraphic Sentence

English grammar applies to your resume, but there are some exceptions:

- The subject of a resume sentence is generally implied rather than expressed.

- The definite article "the" is often omitted. Thus "Bob hit the ball" would be written "Hit ball" in "resume-ese."

- The first person personal pronouns (I, me, my) are almost always omitted.

- The implied subject of a resume sentence is generally in the third person singular (he; she). However some people prefer the implied subject to be "I." Of course in the past tense, (I) Hit and (he) Hit would be rendered "Hit" either way. In the present tense, one form would change: (I) Hit *versus* (he) Hits. Whether you choose first or third person for the implied subject is not critical; being consistent with the choice you make is.

- Since your resume should tell about *you*, your implied subject will seldom be in the plural. Thus, even if you worked as part of a team, your resume should identify what *you* demonstrated achieved or learned. For example: *Reduced overhead by 15% as part of six person company-wide team.*

TIP #11: Distinguish Between Truth and Stupidity

One of our principles is that **everything** you write on your resume must be true. A corollary is that **nothing** you write should undermine your chances for winning an interview. Let's look at an example to distinguish between truth and stupidity.

Truth (Truth Intelligently Presented)	Stupidity (Truth Stupidly Presented)
▪ Decreased defect rate by 10%	▪ Achieved 66% of planned reduction in defect rate
NOTE: In each case, the targeted reduction was 15%	

Decreasing defects is a selling point but partial fulfillment of a goal can work against you.

On a related point, think at least twice before writing something on your resume you wouldn't want to discuss at your interview. For example: If you caused strife with the assembly workers, lost customers through delayed deliveries and increased costs while reducing defects, it may be safer not to mention the reduction in defects at all.

TIP #12: A Terrible Truth: An Awful Resume Sometimes Wins and a Great Resume Often Loses

Picture Corona, a recruiter with two resumes on her desk. The resume from Jill is professional in appearance, well organized and clear in its presentation. Michele's resume shows no great thought given to it but indicates that she is a nuclear physicist and speaks three languages. Whom does Corona choose for the interview?

It depends. In this case Corona is looking for a trilingual nuclear physicist. Jill, a graphic artist, doesn't fit Corona's need, but

Michele might. "I am here to identify job applicants who might meet our needs, not to judge resumes as such," Corona says, "If anyone gets an interview in this case it will be Michele."

A good resume **increases your chances** of winning a job interview, but it provides no guarantee. An awful resume **decreases** your chances but doesn't reduce them to zero.

TIP 13: Don't Drive Yourself Crazy

Write to be within the parameters of what is professionally acceptable. Unless you know the preferences of the specific person reading your resume, don't drive yourself crazy trying to write an absolutely perfect resume. The very notion of a "perfect resume" is dubious. There are two reasons:

- It's impossible to know what a stranger's personal preferences are.

- The goal of the resume reader is to find good people to employ, not to critique resumes.

Beware of Resume Myths

There are lots of myths about resumes which can harm your job search. Let's take a look at some common ones.

TIP #14: The "Showing Accomplishments is Boasting" Myth

Many of us have been taught to be modest and not boastful. That is a wonderful virtue—if we do not confuse presenting your strengths with boasting. Your resume should show the match between your positive characteristics and the employer's needs.

The employer cannot know good things about you unless you write them on your resume.

Presenting your accomplishments becomes boasting only if you are vainglorious or excessive about it. It would be a loss to the employer if s/he didn't interview you because your resume failed to show how good you really are. So if you won't present your strengths for your own sake, do it for the sake of the economy.

Let's look at some examples which distinguish between showing accomplishments and boasting:

Showing Accomplishments	Boasting
■ Employee of the Year Award (1997)	■ Best employee in the company
■ Identified microbe that had escaped detection for three years.	■ Identified elusive microbe other researchers couldn't detect.
■ Reduced defect rate by 20%	■ Beat every other division in company in reducing defects.

TIP #15: Avoid the "Save Something For the Interview" Myth

The main purpose of your resume is to win job interviews in an honest way. Omitting something from your resume to "save it" for your interview is nonsensical for two reasons. First, the toughest part of your job search is getting invited to job interviews in the first place. Leaving out something important reduces your odds of getting invited to the interview. Second, your resume will often be used as a guide for the interviewer in developing his/her questions. An explicit statement on your resume is more likely to be discussed than something which you didn't write.

Lauren's situation provides a case in point. Prior to leaving the work force, she had been promoted four times in three years. When I asked Lauren why she didn't mention that fact on her resume, she said "I wanted to save a real zinger for the interview." After Lauren and I discussed this matter, she decided to include her "zingers" in her resume to maximize the probability of being invited to an interview at all.

TIP #16: Avoid the "Goulash" Myth By Targeting Your Resume

Some people are tempted to load their resume with every conceivable fact. Their theory is "Maybe the resume reader will see something of interest that way." Maybe, but probably not. The goulash resume—which is like a stew with everything imaginable in it—tends to be overly wordy and not clearly organized. Even if you have attractive selling points, they are likely to be overwhelmed by the rest of the stew.

Your resume is more likely to be an attractive dish if it is built around three to five main ingredients (e.g. selling points) than if you throw in the entire kitchen sink. Whetting the recruiter's appetite by showing that you offer characteristics important to the employer is a good idea. Overwhelming the recruiter with lots to read of little relevance to him/her is not.

TIP #17: Avoid the "Copy a Successful Resume" Myth

This book contains numerous examples of good resume ideas. However, I encourage you not to **copy** any of them. Instead, use the examples to prod your own thinking and creativity. Copying someone else's resume, no matter how successful s/he was, can be detrimental to your job search for several reasons:

- The other person may have won job interviews for reasons not related to the quality of his/her resume. This could happen if s/he had easily identifiable skills in high demand or was well known in his/her profession. Most of us are not that fortunate.

- The other person's resume may present wonderful characteristics of no compelling interest to **your** prospective employers.

- Taking the easy road stands in the way of exploring important truths about yourself. A well considered, well presented you is more appealing than an imitation of someone else.

Don't Edit As You Write

Writing anything worth reading can be difficult. Just getting started poses a problem for many people. Once you have planned the basic strategy for your resume, let your pen or word processor roll. Editing for more powerful, concise sentences and to avoid excessive length can come later. We will discuss editing your resume in Chapter 10.

In Chapter 1 we learned some general principles on which to build your resume. In Chapter 2, we will learn how to get started.

2

Getting Started

In this chapter we will look at three steps you should take before you start writing: build at least one inventory of positive characteristics, develop a theme, and plan the use of space.

Build an Inventory of Positive Characteristics

A good first step is to build an inventory of your positive attributes from which you can draw resume material. Broadly speaking, there are three approaches you could take:

➤ **Your Own Positive Characteristics:** A common approach is to examine thoroughly your work experiences and activities, to identify **positive characteristics**, namely skills and attributes, which you possess.

➤ **Generic Characteristics:** Some characteristics are important in many fields. An inventory of such **generic** skills will help you with your resume, cover letter, and interviews.

14

➤ **Specific Characteristics For Your Next Employer:**
An alternate approach is to identify the **specific** characteristics your next employer would need, then match
your positive characteristics with the employer's needs.

Starting with your own positive characteristics has the advantage of being more inclusive. This is an especially good approach
if self reflection is one goal for writing your resume. Generic
inventories help you identify characteristics which are important
but which you may overlook because you think that *"everyone* has
that skill." Starting with the employer's specific needs quickly
focuses on selling points you need to highlight. It is particularly
useful for those who are already clear about their professional
goals and/or want to develop a new resume in fairly short order.

In the next four tips, we will follow members of our Job Search
Club (see pages x-xi) as they utilize each approach. Remember
that many people develop all three inventories.

TIP #18: Your Own Positive Characteristics:
A "Start With Yourself" Inventory

David was an experienced professional who wanted to change to
a new field. Before making such a major step in his life, a self
examination was surely in order. David wanted to identify as many
of his positive characteristics as possible. This is an abbreviated
version of how David used four sources for this inventory:

▪ **Job Description:** David reviewed the job description
for his current position. He noted that a credit analyst at
his bank *"analyzes* data submitted by individuals and
businesses seeking loans; *determines* credit worthiness
and degree of associated *risk, advises* loan committee
on appropriate action in *documented* report." Based on

this part of his job description, David included **analyze, determine risk, advise, document** in his inventory. David wasn't concerned that his inventory was not uniformly one part of speech.

- **Performance Review (PR):** David's performance was reviewed annually by his manager, so David examined his most recent PR's for inventory ideas. His manager had referred to him as **"diligent," "insightful," "thorough,"** and **"highly respected."** David immediately added these characteristics in his inventory. David also noted that his manager was less enthusiastic about David's *volume* of output. This latter point wouldn't make a good resume item, but it did alert David to a topic he might have to address at a job interview.

- **Work Diary:** David started to keep a diary of his daily work life. His purpose was twofold: **First,** he wanted to capture positive characteristics not expressed in his job description or performance review. In writing his diary, David noted that he had to utilize a considerable degree of *subjective judgment* since loan applicants' financial data really didn't provide everything David needed to consider. **Second,** David also noted in his diary what he enjoyed about his job and what he didn't. This information wouldn't provide a resume item, but it might help David identify new career alternatives.

- **Listen to Colleagues:** David listened to his colleagues. From the water cooler talk with other credit analysts, David realized that internal politics were an integral part of the job. "I would think more than twice before recommending against a loan request from a crucial client," one of his colleagues mentioned. David thought about this comment and put a positive spin on it: "Considers the larger goals of the organization" was added to David's inventory.

TIP #19: Generic Inventory: Identify *Generic* Characteristics Many Employers Might Want

Some characteristics would be appealing to most employers irrespective of the specific position which is to be filled. For example:

- Leadership
- Organizing
- Communications
- Problem Solving
- Hard working
- Reliable
- Self-starting
- Intellectual Curiosity
- Team Player

The degree to which each of these characteristics is important will vary according to the situation, so simply loading these characteristics on your resume is probably not a good idea. We will explore stressing the most important characteristics for a specific resume goal later.

TIP #20: A *Specific* Characteristics Inventory

There are characteristics which may be important in one job but far less important (or even undesirable) in another. Let's listen as two members of the Job Search Club discuss specific characteristics for their next job.

Rhonda is a business professional seeking to move up in her current profession, marketing. She knew from experience that the ability to analyze marketing data was critical to her success. Rhonda also knew from discussions with peers that a healthy respect for budgetary constraints was essential. Successful people in her field were flexible, but decisive, a balance sometimes difficult to maintain. Rhonda wrote **analyze, budget conscious, flexible, decisive** in her specific inventory, realizing that she could add more characteristics later.

Gabrielle, a budding microbiologist, also started to develop her inventory of specific characteristics. A thorough knowledge of microscopic organisms, their characteristics and growth, was clearly essential. Given Gabrielle's particular interest in Talking Horse Syndrome (THS) a knowledge of the relationship between organisms and disease, in addition to the effects of antibiotics on microorganisms, was quite important. Like Rhonda, Gabrielle needed analytical skills, albeit they would be applied to scientific, rather than marketing data. Gabrielle began her inventory of specific characteristics with: **Knowledge of microorganisms; relationship between organisms and disease; analytical.**

In the Tip which follows, we will look at a necessary next step: Developing examples to validate the positive characteristics in your inventories.

TIP #21: Use Examples to Validate
Your Inventory of Characteristics

Picture Larry and his twin brother Barry discussing their resumes. Which presentation seems more convincing to you?

Barry wrote: Problem Solver

Larry wrote: Solved problems ranging from absentee-
ism to stock shrinkage.

Most people would find Larry's presentation more credible
because he has provided an example. Your resume requires an
honest **presentation**, not **proof** as in a court of law. If you are
invited to an interview, the employer can probe your characteristics more thoroughly. A good way to develop examples is to build
a sentence for each characteristic with the personal pronoun "I"
being understood. For example:

(I) **persuaded** manager of another department to drop his
objections to my marketing plan.

Let's look at some examples to support both generic and
specific characteristics. The wording in the chart below does not
have to be in resume form since its purpose is to record ideas for
your later use.

CHARACTERISTIC	EXAMPLE
Hard Working	Worked an average of 60 hours per week to meet deadlines.
Organization	Organized annual meetings, including presentations, promotional literature and conference logistics.
Communication	▪ Wrote manual for new employees describing company philosophy, operating policies, rights and obligations ▪ Presented new product design to board of directors, utilizing Powerpoint visuals, detailed charts and appropriate humor.
Analytical	▪ Analyzed laboratory data to identify possible correlation between smog levels and verbosity. ▪ Analyzed census data to determine which demographic categories were best candidates for new deluxe edition of mature products.

Knowledge of microorganisms	▪ Earned degree in microbiology from top ranked University. ▪ Researched impact of antibiotics on microorganisms while at Cellmate.
Flexibility	Demonstrated flexibility by incorporating interests of four departments into master marketing plan.
Decisive	Decided to pursue Tough Toenail product and development despite ambiguous data and conflicting departmental input.
Empathy	Empathized with employees concerned over job loss, but still instituted efficiency programs.
Initiative	Initiated research on alternative health care packages.
Persuasion	▪ Persuaded management committee that displacing workers with machines would be very expensive in the long run. ▪ Persuaded reluctant staff member to try a new approach.
Integrity	▪ Recognized for integrity by receiving "Employee of the Year" Award. ▪ Accepted potentially unpleasant consequences from signing off on data which conflicted with the prevailing view.
Time Management	▪ Completed all projects on or before schedule. ▪ Managed project involving contingent processes and uncertain lead times. ▪ Achieved excellent grades while working 30 hours a week.

Uncovering Important Characteristics
For Your Inventory

In the previous four tips we discussed building inventories of your positive characteristics. The following three Tips suggest sources for identifying those characteristics.

TIP #22: Information Interviews

One way to find out what it takes to do a specific job well is to ask people who are doing it. A common name for this method is an information interview. It is particularly appropriate for Larry, a college senior, Lauren who is returning to the workforce and David who hopes to take the next step in his current career. Rhonda may find that less formal means of gathering information are more appropriate. Business lunches, professional conferences and her observations of more senior managers would be examples.

TIP #23: Help Wanted Ads Can Be an Inventory Building Source

You can make good use of help wanted notices in building your specific characteristics inventory since these ads usually contain a statement of skills and attributes the particular employer wants. Let's take a look at a hypothetical example.

Help Wanted Advertisement

Financial Advisors

A rapidly growing, highly reputable financial services firm is seeking talented professionals to join its staff of financial advisors. Excellent analytical and interpersonal skills required. Integrity a must. Previous financial services experience highly desirable.

Respond to Box 4321
Covington Clarion

A person reading this help wanted notice could add **analytical, interpersonal skills and integrity** to his/her specific skills inventory for a financial advisor. It is also helpful to note what is **not** said. For example, no specific college degree or major is required. That could be important to a college senior, a career changer or a person returning to the work force, as they consider their professional options.

TIP #24: Reference Books

There are a number of books which are useful for building inventories of positive characteristics needed in various professions. An outstanding example is:

> *Occupational Outlook Handbook (OOH)*
> (U.S. Department of Labor)

You should be able to find many useful career books in your school or public library and in local bookstores. You also can order many such resources by using the form at the back of this book or by visiting Impact Publications' online career bookstore: *http://www.impactpublications.com*

The *OOH* includes articles about hundreds of professions. Each article includes a paragraph or two about skills needed in that profession. This is the source Gabrielle used in Tip #20, but the other Job Search Club members could have used it as well.

Professional Associations often have free or inexpensive literature about their field. An excellent source to identify professional associations relevant for you is the *Encyclopedia of Associations* published by Gale Research.

TIP #25: Develop a Theme

Develop a one line theme which contains the message that you want your resume to deliver. Your theme will help you stay focused as you craft your resume and it may serve as a basis for writing a summary (see Tip #32). Here are some themes developed by members of our Job Search Club:

Rhonda: *Marketing professional with 10+ year track record in consumer goods.*

Gabrielle: *Well trained microbiologist with extensive laboratory experience.*

David: *Finance professional with excellent analytical and decision-making skills.*

Lauren: *Effective manager. Demonstrated organizational and innovative skills.*

Larry: *Hardworking, realistic college graduate.*

In this chapter we learned how and why to build inventories of your positive characteristics. In Chapter 3 we will look at planning before you write.

3

Planning Before You Write

Before you start writing your resume, it is important to plan the use of space. Planning is the topic of this chapter.

Planning the Use of Space

Here is a **general principle** for utilizing your one page of resume space.

The greater the importance, the greater the prominence.

The implication for space as such is that the more important the text, the more space should be allocated to it.

TIP #26: The Amount of Space
Depends On the Degree of Importance

Rhonda has held three jobs in the last ten years. In her initial resume draft, she devoted six lines to her first job, two lines to her second job and four lines to her current position. Her rationale was this: "I spent five years at Firstco, and that's where I started my career. The job at Secondco lasted only two years, and then I moved on to Currentco."

I pointed out to Rhonda that she had allocated resume space based on **longevity**, a significant mistake. She would be better advised to allocate space based on the significance of the experience for selling her candidacy to an employer. Putting our principle into practice, Rhonda now gave the most space to her current job. That made sense because her position with Currentco provided the best reason for a prospective employer to be interested in her. Rhonda's first job, on the other hand, was old news by now. Although it held a warm place in Rhonda's heart, that first job would not likely be of great interest to future employers. Therefore, Rhonda decided to devote only two or three lines to it.

Put yourself in a recruiter's place and look at the schema below. Notice how your attention focuses on the job experience which occupies the most space. Think of this schema when allocating space on your resume.

Currentco—Manager of Planning

Secondco—Director of Forecasting
Firstco—Planning Analyst

Visibility and the logic of your resume should be closely related. Logically speaking, major items should be more visible than relatively minor ones. Additional tools for linking logic and visibility are organization and location. Let's take a look at each in the following two tips.

TIP #27: Organization: Always Logical, Not Necessarily Chronological

The first job you mention should be a stronger selling point than other jobs on your resume. Put your best foot first, not in the middle. For some people, like Rhonda, her current job is the strongest because it presents Rhonda in her highest level of authority. Since Rhonda is staying within her current profession, a **chronological resume**, with current job first, makes sense.

David is in a different situation. He is trying to change either the type of work he does or the industry he is in, and perhaps both. For David, subdividing his resume into important categories is a good idea. The first category would contain his strongest selling point. For David, a **category resume** makes the most sense. Let's take a look at some possible categories for David.

David is currently a credit analyst at a commercial bank. Previously he had worked as a sales representative of a computer data storage company. If David were seeking a position as a financial analyst in a high tech company, the schema of his experience might look like this to show experience in the high tech industry:

PROFESSIONAL EXPERIENCE

Technology
Gizmo Computer Storage Device, Bethesda, MD.

Financial
Credit Commercial Bank, Fairfax, VA.

If David wanted to emphasize his financial experience, he could reverse the categories.

PROFESSIONAL EXPERIENCE

Financial
Credit Commercial Bank, Fairfax, VA.

Technology
Gizmo Computer Storage Device, Bethesda, MD.

Larry, a college senior, is also drafting his resume. Currently, he is a library clerk on campus. During the previous summer he worked for a market research firm, albeit in a mundane capacity. If Larry is applying for a position in Market Research, the schema for his Experience might look like this:

EXPERIENCE

Market Research
Consumer Consensus Associates, Brockton, MA.

Administrative
Mt. Herman Library, South Hadley, MA

If Larry had been president of his fraternity, his Experience could look like this:

EXPERIENCE

Market Research
Consumer Consensus Associates   Brockton, MA

Leadership
President, Alpha Beta Gamma Fraternity   South Hadley, MA

Administrative
Mt. Herald Library   South Hadley, MA

TIP #28: Location

A rough rule of thumb about location is that sooner is better than later. For example, if your work experience is a major selling point, it should come before your Education. A recent college graduate like Larry would reverse the order. As a corollary, each statement under any specific work experience should be at least as important to a prospective employer as the one which follows it. Let's look at an example:

David looked at his inventory and noted some of his positive characteristics which would be important to an appropriate recruiter. This was the order of the verbs in David's draft resume:

- Communicated ...

- Analyzed ...

- Researched ...

- Organized ...

I asked David which of the four points would be most important to the recruiter. David responded by saying "Research, and see, it is right here on the draft." "You're half-right" I said to David. "But the first point is sure to be read, the third point may not be." David wasn't completely convinced. "But I spent more time communicating than researching," David protested. **"Remember that your resume is intended to show that you have the skills for your next job, not to capture an exact picture of a present or past job,"** I responded. Seeing the logic of this Tip, David reorganized his verbs, putting "Researched" first.

An exception to our general rule: The last item on your resume can be a choice location. That would be a good place for a statement like "Willing to relocate," if that would be an important consideration, or "Permanent Resident of the United States" if something on your resume might suggest that you have a visa problem.

In Chapter 3, we learned some tips for planning your resume. Starting with Chapter 4, we will take a look at four main sections of your resume.

4

Heading

The heading of your resume is something of a paradox. It is the **least** important part in terms of the decision whether or not to interview you. On the other hand, it contains the **vital information** a recruiter would need to contact you if s/he wished to. Let's look at a few tips about headings.

TIP #29: Stick to the Basics

Your name, home address and home phone are critical. A work phone number suggests your permission to call you at work, so think twice before providing it. Many people today include an e-mail address. If that address is at your place of work, make sure that e-mail use for private purposes does not violate company policy and that your e-mail is secure from access by anyone but you.

A typical heading could look like this:

MATTHEW MANGALISO

1776 Heritage Drive
Minneapolis, MN 55402
(612) 794-3719 (H)
(612) 431-1673 (W)
e-mail: mmangaliso@cmpactco.com

It is a good idea to skip a line between your name and home address, but it is not absolutely necessary. There is no requirement to type your name in a larger font than your address, but it can be a good idea if space permits. If space is tight, you could put both your home phone number and work phone number on the same line, like this: (612) 794-3719 (H); (612) 431-1673 (W).

TIP #30: A Case of Two Addresses

Sometimes it makes sense to have two addresses in your heading, particularly if you are a forthcoming college graduate. One address would be your current or college address and the other would be your permanent or home address. The purpose of the second address is to provide a means of contacting you when you are not at college. A college student's heading might look like this:

Brenna O'Casey

College Address	**Permanent Address**
43651 Palm Drive	14 Longhorn Drive
San Bernardino, CA 92401	Dallas, TX 78760
(909) 894-6673	(214) 379-9743
bocasey@emeritus.ucsb.edu	

TIP #31: Omitting Information

There may be times that you will want to omit information from
your heading. Many job seekers do this because of the following
reasons:

- **Personal Security.** Some people choose to leave off their
  address for reasons of personal security. Instead, they
  indicate a post office box. Similarly, a job applicant may
  not wish to reveal a home phone number. A work phone,
  an e-mail address or even a friend's phone number could
  be used instead. Such situations are relatively rare, but
  you could have a heading like this one:

> **Jennifer Rodgers**
>
> P.O. Box 1797
> Philadelphia, PA 19152
> (215) 794-1932

Use of a post office box is likely to raise questions in the
mind of employers. Some employers assume if an applicant does not list a street address s/he has something to
hide or is transient. Make sure your reason for not using
a street address outweighs potential negatives this may
convey to employers.

- **Avoid raising a geographic barrier.** Let's say that you
  are a college senior who was raised in Kentucky, attended
  college in Indiana and plans to seek a position in Arizona.
  Instead of providing a home or permanent address, simply
  indicate the appropriate phone numbers. That minimizes

giving addresses in two states, neither of which is Arizona. Your heading might look like this:

> Joseph Green
> 17 Hoosier Boulevard
> South Bend, Indiana
> (606) 439-2741
> (219) 761-1893

5

Consider a Summary Statement

TIP #32: A Good Summary Is Usually an Asset

A short statement indicating specific positive characteristics of value to your prospective employer is often helpful. This statement could go under the title "Summary," "Objective," "Skill Summary," or "Qualifications." These and similar terms vary slightly in their nuances, but for ease of presentation, we will use the term "Summary" in the text of this book. The important thing is to match what the employer needs with positive characteristics you offer. In addition, a sentence identifying the next step in your career is appropriate unless you are writing a purely generic resume or your career objective is self evident from the rest of your resume.

Picture yourself reading a newspaper. There is a good chance that you will read the headline preceding an article prior to reading the story itself. The headline gives you a general sense of what the article is about and may shape your perception of what you subsequently read. A headline may also influence your decision whether even to read the article or not.

In many situations, a Summary is like a newspaper headline. Your Summary provides a chance to achieve two goals quickly: To say some job related things about yourself which are important to the prospective employer; to indicate a professional goal which is consistent with a staffing need of the employer.

Here are some examples:

SUMMARY: Seven years experience in export/import. Demonstrated expertise in building client base. Conversant in three languages. Seeks to continue career in larger organization.

OBJECTIVE: Seeks position in corporate treasury function where analytical, research and reporting skills will contribute to company's profitability.

SKILL SUMMARY: Excellent writing, research, time management skills. Three years experience in consumer product packaging.

The titles in the three examples above could be interchanged with no loss to your resume.

Sometimes you may wish to be even more tightly aligned with the needs of an employer. For example: a person seeking a financial position in a *multi-division firm* could write

---

QUALIFICATIONS FOR FINANCE POSITION

Five years experience analyzing financial statements and cash flows. Earned CFA in 1998. Enhanced interest earnings and reduced debt by implementing uniform financial practices throughout multi-division firm.

Some people use a two-tier statement like the one below:

OBJECTIVE:　　Sales position in the widget industry.
QUALIFIED BY:
- Four years as widget buyer.
- Wide spread professional network built as Vice President of National Widget Association.
- Excellent time management, presentation and negotiation skills.

TIP #33: Key Words

One approach to a Summary is to have a section of "Key Words". Key Words comprise your major skills and attributes in *noun* form.

The use of Key Words has been recommended for resumes which will be scanned by an Optical Character Reader (OCR) and stored in a database. A major rationale is that OCR's have been able to read nouns better than verbs. A related reason is to provide an opportunity to use synonyms for the positive characteristics which you present in the rest of your resume. Using synonyms increases the number of potential "hits" on your resume when the database is searched in response to a job requisition. The job description or help wanted ads often provide a good source of words for your Key Words sentences as well as other sections of your resume.

OCR's are becoming more sophisticated, so they are increasingly able to read verbs as well as nouns. However, the idea behind Key Words is still useful, especially if you know your resume is going to be scanned. Your Key Words section might look like the one below.

> **Key Words:** Writing, Research, Management, Designing, Persuasion, Negotiation, Organization

Other names for a section like this are "Major Attributes," "Qualifications" or something identified with the prospective job such as "Marketing Skills."

TIP #34: Deciding If a Summary Is Helpful

To continue with our headline analogy, sometimes you choose **not** to read an article because the headline doesn't attract you or even turns you off. There is some risk that a Summary might also have a negative effect. Here are some rules of thumb to determine how beneficial a summary might be for you:

Summary definitely advisable: If you are a recent college graduate, a career changer or returning to the work force, your career goal is probably not self evident from your work experience. Neither are your applicable skills and characteristics. Instead, you are about to embark on a new professional path. A Summary conveys the message that you know what characteristics are important in that job. It also says that you do indeed have a career goal and that you are not merely looking for a paycheck.

Summary not critical: If you are continuing on the same functional career path, your applicable skills and career direction are apparent from your work experience.

Summary not advisable: If you have no idea about the needs of those who may read your resume, and/or have no idea about your career goals, a Summary could work against you. In general, a poorly stated Summary can be worse than no Summary at all.

Summary definitely advisable	Summary not critical	Summary not advisable
▪ recent college graduate ▪ changing career ▪ returning to workforce	▪ continuing functional career path	▪ generic resume; interests of recipients not known; your career goals cannot be articulated at all.

TIP #35: Better to Give Than to Receive

A general principle about Summaries: It is better to give than to receive. Therefore, begin by presenting what you can give your next employer. Then, indicate what you want, such as "seeks to build a career in financial analysis."

Making demands on the prospective employer can be counterproductive. Gabrielle's first draft summary provides an example:

> "Experienced microbiologist with demonstrated research and project management skills. Seeks position where utilizing sophisticated equipment and techniques will yield further advances in the field of science; particularly in regard to Talking Horse Syndrome (THS)."

A potential pitfall for Gabrielle is that she has expressed a demand on the employer, namely a work environment "utilizing sophisticated equipment and techniques." It would have been better to express that thought in terms of what Gabrielle *can give*:

> **"Competent with even the most sophisticated equipment and techniques."**

A related problem for Gabrielle, at least potentially, is her desire for "further advances in the field of science." This would make sense in a pure research situation. However, in a more commercial environment, it is business needs which set the research agenda. Similarly, Gabrielle's specific interest in Talking Horse Syndrome would be an asset only if the employer is interested in THS. Otherwise, Gabrielle's expressed interest in THS could become an albatross around the neck of Gabrielle's resume.

TIP #36: Link Your Summary and Experience

A headline is connected to the story which follows. In a similar way, your summary should be connected to the rest of your resume, especially the Experience section. Refer to the "Skill Summary" example in Tip #32. Help the resume reader believe that you have "excellent writing, research and time management skills. Three years experience in consumer product packaging" by demonstrating these characteristics. An abbreviated example is found on page 40.

In this chapter, we saw the value of a Summary and how to construct one. The next chapter will discuss your Experience section.

EXPERIENCE
CONSUMER PRODUCT PACKAGING (1995-present)

Huddle Horend, Inc. (1997-present)
Director of Research

■ Researched cost effective ways to utilize sturdy, safe materials for wrapping toys. Identified combination which saved firm $8 million.

■ Wrote proposals resulting in new approaches for decorating toy cartons and utilizing boxes which reduced shipping losses.

Cavity Toothpaste Company (1995-1997)
Project Manager

■ Managed multiple projects simultaneously, bringing each to completion before deadline.

6

Experience

Your "Experience" section provides an opportunity to present your **positive characteristics**, namely skills and attributes you have demonstrated, achieved or learned. Of most importance are those positive characteristics which would be valuable to your next employer. Experience is generally presented within the framework of jobs you have had for three reasons: First, to give structure to your presentation. Second, to lend credibility to what you present. Third, performance on past jobs is often seen as a predictor of future job performance.

Avoid falling into the trap of simply describing past or present *jobs*. Instead describe *you*. Show through your past or current accomplishments that *you* have the positive characteristics to accomplish important objectives for your *next* employer.

TIP #37: Give Clear Reasons For a Response of "Yes"

For your resume to be effective it must convey quickly and clearly good reasons to interview you. Good reasons would include skills

41

and attributes needed by the employer in a specific industry and/or functional experience similar to the employer's needs.

Let's follow some of our Job Search Club members as they identify reasons for an employer to say "yes."

Lauren is interested in returning to the work force. Prior to starting her family, Lauren worked for a not-for-profit charitable organization. "I enjoyed many aspects of what I did," Lauren said, "but I think that for the hours I put in I could be better compensated in the for-profit sector."

Based on information interviews and ideas she gleaned from the *Occupational Outlook Handbook*, Lauren was exploring several career possibilities. One of these was Health Service Management.

Lauren's notes indicated that a health service manager "plans, organizes and coordinates the delivery of health care." Public speaking, promotion participation and complying with government regulations might also be important parts of the job." Lauren compared these characteristics with her own inventory of positive characteristics (see Tip #18) and realized that she could give an employer in Health Service Management a number of good reasons to say yes. This is part of what Lauren wrote in her "Experience" section:

MANAGEMENT EXPERIENCE
Administrative Manager
Singing for At-Risk Children, Detroit, MI

     Planned annual conferences for individual and corporate sponsors. Organized concert tours of at-risk children served by foundation. Spoke to civic and media gatherings to promote SARC. Complied with government regulations and detailed by-laws while building 600 client organization.

TIP #38: Avoid Giving Reasons For Saying "No"

These would include wrong focus, and "button pushers" like frequent job changes and absence from the work force. Let's look at
some examples:

Wrong Focus:

If you have a career objective on your resume (see Tip #32),
make sure it is at least related to the job for which you are
applying. For example, a marketing objective makes no
sense for a resume sent to a Controller (who would look for
accountants). If you are interested in a career change, like
David, you can minimize this problem with a little fore-
thought and creativity.

Button Pushers:

- **Poor Appearance:** This includes illogical construction
  and sloppy spacing. For ways to avoid these pitfalls, see
  Tip #26 and Tip #27.

- **Misspelled words and poor grammar:** Using the "spell-
  check" on your word processor is not enough. Use a
  dictionary to double check any word on which you would-
  n't bet your mortgage. Also, read your resume from
  bottom up, in reverse order. This approach will help you
  see what you actually wrote down, which is often distinct
  from what you intended. Intelligent formatting can often
  avoid these problems.

Overly long:

For many people one page is the proper length. Longer
resumes tend to bury useful information on the second page,
where it is less likely to have impact. As a general principle,
if it's important, it belongs on page 1; if it's not important,
why do you need to include it? An overly long resume sends
the message that you can't establish and present your
priorities. That perception could seriously hurt your chance
for an interview.

Here is a good rule of thumb if determining whether your
resume should be one or two pages:

For many people, particularly those early in their career, a
one page resume makes the most sense. On the other hand,
if you have a significant amount of work experience with
clear relevance to a prospective employer, a two page
resume is often desirable. This book gives examples of both
one and two page resumes so you can decide which serves
your job search strategy better. If you remain doubtful,
choose a one page resume.

A Useful Exercise: Play Your Strongest Hand

Every individual has a large number of positive characteristics.
Your resume can deliver a message about a small sub-set of them,
perhaps four or five. How do you identify those characteristics
which are the best selling points?

We already learned how to identify characteristics needed to
succeed in a particular field (Tip #19). Your **second** step is to
identify those characteristics the employer needs that you can fill
(Tip #20). In this Tip you will learn how to identify four or five

characteristics the employer needs where you are particularly strong by playing the Strongest Hand. This is a card game which forces you to identify your most important characteristics for each job search situation you will face. For example, Harry is interested in pursuing a career in marketing management. Utilizing the sources noted in Tips #22-24, Harry compiles a list of ten important characteristics needed in a market manager. Of these, Harry matched seven with his own positive characteristics. But Harry knew that his resume would be more powerful if it focused only on four (maximum five). What did Harry do?

Harry wrote each of the seven matching characteristics on a "playing card"—really a 3"x5" index card. He shuffled the deck and dealt himself four cards. Then Harry picked one card at a time from the remaining deck. Harry had to decide if each new card was more powerful than any already in his hand. If "yes," Harry replaced the weakest card in his hand with the new card. If "no," the new card was put aside. Harry repeated the process for each card in the deck. At the end of the process, each of Harry's seven characteristics had been weighed against the rest and only the strongest four were retained.

But how did Harry determine which characteristics were relatively stronger? There are two criteria to use:

- What is most significant to the employer;
- Characteristics for which Harry has the strongest **examples**.

Based on reading useful references, his own related experiences and information interviews (Tip #22), Harry assigned each card a **value to the employer** using this scale:

3 points = extremely important
2 points = strong

1 point = useful, not critical

Next, Harry allocated points to each of **his positive character-istics** based on the quality of the example(s) he could give to validate his statement.

3 points = extremely strong
2 points = strong
1 point = true statement, but not all that impressive

In this way, Harry could assign a value to each of his character-istics by combining the employer's points and his own points.

Let's look at an example. Harry looked at the four cards he had drawn. Harry knew that from an employer's point of view communication skills are extremely important in marketing managers (3 points). Harry had a good example of written communication but is only fair in his oral delivery. He added 2 more points for a total of 5. Previously, Harry had assigned a value to "creativity" (2 points + 1 point = 3 points), and to marketing experience in that industry (3 pints + 3 points = 6 points), and team building (2 points + 2 points = 4 points). Harry now ranked his cards in this order: Marketing experience in that industry, Communication, Team Building and Creativity.

Harry now picked a fifth card from his deck. If the positive characteristic of that card was assigned more than 3 points in value, Harry added it to his hand of four strongest positive charac-teristic cards and discarded creativity. Harry continued the process with the remaining positive characteristic cards in his deck.

TIP #39: Address Doubts

Sometimes a resume raises doubts in the mind of the recruiter. Try to alleviate such doubts by anticipating what they might be and developing a solution. The chart below provides some examples:

Situation	Doubt	Solution
Returning to Work Force	Out of Touch	Recent use of Positive Characteristics; some computer literacy; membership in appropriate professional association
Changing fields	Malcontent, failed	Success in field; professional awards
Recent college graduate	unrealistic expectations; unfocused	hardworking; work during academic year; co-op or internship; clear Summary

Some of our Job Search Club members applied this Tip to themselves. Lauren, who was returning to the work force after a number of years, realized that her two recent temporary positions would help overcome the concern that she was out of touch. "Even if I didn't need those jobs for income, temp work would be worth it for resume purposes alone," Lauren thought to herself. Lauren also made sure to include mention of her computer literacy, in her case use of EXCEL and Lotus. "Professional memberships would help me become more current if I actively participated." Lauren realized "When my career goals become more focused, that is something I will definitely pursue."

David thought about his situation: "I want to leave banking even though I am doing well in professional terms. Last year I was sent to the American Bankers Association and made a brief presentation. That should help. Maybe a positive comment from my annual performance review might be useful as well," he reasoned. (See Tip #21).

Larry considered some of the stereotypes about recent college graduates. "I will make sure to mention that I worked 20 hours a week during the academic year and paid for 90% of my living expenses. That should show I am hard working and responsible. In my Summary, I will make sure to state a clear career goal to show a focus, even if that means a different resume for each of the different kinds of positions I may pursue. I didn't have a co-op as such, but I can indicate a realistic sense of what work is. There was nothing glamorous about the jobs I held, but I did learn how to 'play office' and that's an asset."

TIP #40: Think Broadly About "Experience"

Sometimes people think that "Experience" applies only to paid employment. It is perfectly legitimate to think more broadly.

- **Volunteer experience** may have given you an opportunity to develop good skills in communication, leadership, organization or teamwork. Presenting such volunteer experience under "Experience" makes sense, especially if you cannot show those skills in paid situations. Lauren's case provides a good example:

Lauren has been out of the work force for a number of years while raising a family. She utilized her experience as vice-president of the local Parent-Teacher Organization (PTO) to demonstrate her organizational ability and familiarity with computers.

> **Vice President – Happy Valley PTO, Michigan** (1996-98)
> Organized fund raising campaign which yielded $250,000 in labor, materials and cash for a new recreation facility. Persuaded local merchants to donate material in exchange for good will. Researched fund raising techniques using the Internet and created EXCEL file of contributors.

Once Lauren starts her next paying job, she could reposition her PTO experience as an OSP (Other Selling Point), perhaps under the banner of Civic Organizations, or delete it entirely.

- Unpaid internships and some class assignments may provide valuable experiences for college students. For example, Larry, a recent college graduate, included this text under Experience in one of his resumes.

> **National Saw & Chain – Agawam, MA**
> Surveyed employees to identify perceptions of fringe benefits package. Designed questionnaire to maximize response rate while capturing critical facts. Analyzed data to identify patterns and potential problems. Reported to Vice President on conclusions and recommendations (Internship – Fall 1997)

TIP #41: Make Good Use of Temporary Work

People use temporary employment services, sometimes referred to as "Temp Agencies" for several reasons:

- **A stop gap** measure to provide income while looking for a new job.

- **A short term job** when only a limited amount of time is available.

- **As a foot in the door** for a permanent position, some companies utilize the period a temporary employee is with them as a screening tool. In such cases, temporary employment may grow into a full-time permanent career position.

- **To re-activate** a resume after a period outside the work force.

Some people feel that "temp work" is somehow unworthy of mention on a resume. However, the fact that you may have been underpaid, underutilized or unappreciated is beside the point. If the experience helps you present a selling point, it belongs on your resume.

Sometimes people identify their employer as the temp agency rather than the place where they worked. It is more helpful to both you and the recruiter if the temp agency is mentioned but the place of employment is more prominent. Let's take a look at an example:

Very Good Product, Inc. – Haventown, PA
Excellent Eateries – Media, PA
Demonstrated flexibility by moving among six different functional areas to substitute for vacationing employees. Responded to customer inquiries, built files in EXCEL and developed basic financial reports using Lotus. Learned about specific business concerns in office supply and restaurant industries (1997).
Worked through Ajax Temporary Skilled Workers.

TIP #42: Using a Banner Statement

As Rhonda was drafting her resume, she considered starting the text related to her current position this way:

Three years of increasingly responsible experience with this $600 million consumer products firm.

Then Rhonda proceeded with a presentation of her positive characteristics. I refer to this approach as using a banner statement, although other terminology could be used as well. For Rhonda there were two benefits to this approach:

- It presented a major selling point (e.g., experience in the field) clearly and quickly.

- Rhonda explained two important facts about her employer (size, line of business) which might otherwise have been unknown to a recruiter.

Gabrielle applied the same idea to one of her work experiences:

Researched potential solutions to dioxin contamination as part of team utilizing latest equipment made available by Du Frer Corporation.

The benefits of this banner statement for Gabrielle were:

- A quick statement of her overall experience. This put some of the details which followed in a more under-standable context.

- Indicated a knowledge of dioxin, a major concern in her

field and one with significant commercial implications.

- A statement of team work.

- An indication of experience with the latest related technology.

Larry thought about a banner statement for his resume. A main point he wanted to make was his work ethic:

Worked 20 hours a week, evenings and weekends, to finance college education.

That statement conveys a very positive characteristic. It is much more relevant and powerful than a description of what Larry's duties were—washing dishes.

If you are considering a banner statement, ask yourself if the same thought might be expressed in your Summary. In most cases, you won't need it in both places.

TIP #43: Start Each "Sentence" With a Verb Which Conveys a Positive Characteristic

A good resume writing principle is that sooner is stronger than later. Therefore it makes sense to start each "sentence" with a word which best represents the positive characteristic your prospective employer needs. In most cases, verbs are your best part of speech for that purpose. For example:

- "Wrote reports..." implies the ability to write.

Let's look at some characteristics and match each with a verb:

CHARACTERISTIC	APPROPRIATE VERB
Good at Research	**Researched** market data...
Creative	**Initiated** plan... **Developed** new layouts **Created** new approach
Persuasive	**Persuaded** customers to order drinks **Presented** proposals...

However, some verbs *do not* indicate a positive characteristic needed for your next job:

- "**Performed** audits on a client to determine..." Not bad, but are you trying to convey the characteristic of performing, like a singer or athlete? It is better to get straight to your positive characteristic:

"Audited clients to determine..."

- "**Conducted** survey..." Do you want to conduct an orchestra or conduct electricity? Probably not. Go straight to your positive characteristic. "Surveyed..."

Two notes: First, use verbs in the present tense if the activity is on-going at your current employer. For actions which occurred during past experiences, use the past tense. If in doubt, use the past tense exclusively. Second, sometimes the verb "**learned**" or "**demonstrated**" is appropriate even though you are not trying to convey your capacity to learn or demonstrate as such. This might be the case for a recent college graduate or someone reflecting on an early job. For example:

- **Learned** how different areas of the trading function operate.

- **Demonstrated** good time-management skills by ...

Here are some verbs which may help keep you convey a positive characteristic:

accelerated	improved
accomplished	inspected
adapted	launched
administered	led
analyzed	managed
conceived	mastered
completed	motivated
controlled	operated
coordinated	originated
created	organized
delegated	performed
designed	planned
developed	pinpointed
directed	produced
effected	programmed
eliminated	proved
established	provided
evaluated	purchased
expanded	recommended
expedited	reduced
facilitated	reinforced
generated	reorganized
increased	revised
implemented	reviewed
initiated	scheduled

simplified	surpassed
solved	trained
structured	translated
streamlined	utilized
supervised	won
supported	wrote

TIP #44: One Sentence, One Verb

Your resume will be more powerful if each sentence begins with
one verb, rather than a string of two or three. If you use more than
one verb, your resume will suffer from one of these problems:

- **Cannibalism:** If the verbs are close in meaning, they
  tend to cannibalize rather than strengthen each other. For
  example:

  "Reported and recommended solutions for employee
  training gaps which caused defects."

  The two verbs are so close that neither delivers its full
  power. A piece of "reported" is absorbed by "recommended" and vice-versa. The same idea could be better
  stated this way:

  **"Reported to senior management on solutions to
  employee training gaps. Recommended cost-effective program which reduced defects by 70%."**

Unless you wanted to stress your relationship to senior
management, the sentence starting with "reported" could even be
dropped.

■ **Confusion:** The resume reader needs to know quickly and unambiguously what your sentence means. Multiple verbs can cause confusion. For example:

"Planned and reorganized staff..."

In this case, David has two verbs and one direct object. Did he really mean that he planned the staff? Perhaps David meant that he planned the division's long term goals and reorganized his staff accordingly. The reader cannot be sure.

■ **Attention:** Presenting each verb separately gives each positive characteristic more attention. For example, instead of "Supervised and scheduled part time employees..." You could write:

"Supervised staff of 24. Scheduled part-timers to cover surges in customer traffic."

TIP #45: Third Party Endorsements

Sometimes you can strengthen your resume by including a third party endorsement. (It is the **third** party because it doesn't come from you or the person reading your resume). Let's look at a few examples.

Larry, a recent college graduate, wants his Experience section to convey the high quality of his character. "My work experience is a series of survival jobs. The skills I demonstrated are just not enough," Larry reasoned. For this reason Larry included a sentence like those below in every work experience he presented:

- Praised by manager for hard work and reliability.
- Commended for bringing enthusiasm and fresh ideas to the job.
- Noted by customers for fast, friendly, effective service.

Lauren used similar sentences in describing her experiences prior to leaving the work force and while performing voluntary services in a civic association.

- Promoted four times in five years due to outstanding organization skills.

- Elected President of Royal Bear Civic Association because of excellent managerial and leadership skills.

Rhonda, on the other hand, was seeking to move forward in her current profession. A third party testimonial would add credibility to her resume if she cited a respected source. Therefore, Rhonda developed the following list of sentences to be inserted under appropriate circumstances:

- "Her creativity is matched by her skill in precise implementation. Rhonda has enabled us to cut the lead time in bringing products to market by six months" (1997 Annual Performance Review).

- "Rhonda has been a critical factor in returning our division to profitability." William Tiller, Vice President of Widget Home Appliance division.

Rhonda could locate these sentences in her Summary section, or prior to her Experience section, or with her presentation of the appropriate work experience. Rhonda was aware that some employers would prefer to deal with statements of this type during a reference check. "All things considered, statements of this type might help me and probably wouldn't hurt me," Rhonda concluded.

TIP #46: Active Voice and Unambiguous Meaning

Use verbs in the *active* voice so the reader can learn about **you**. Compare the following:

Increased profits by 10%

vs.

Profits were increased by 10%

The first sentence is about *you* through one of your accomplishments. The second is a statement about profits which says nothing specific about you.

Be careful about using verbs which could be understood in more than one sense. For example: "Consulted clients about more efficient use of existing recycling system." The use of "consulted" is unclear. The reader may think you meant "*conferred*" with clients, "that is, you shared ideas with them. If you meant that the clients paid you for consultation services it would be clearer to write '*advised*' clients about..."

On a related point, write simply. Your resume is going to be read quickly. Avoid complicated constructions like this: *Not only ...but also*. This correlative conjunction is fine for essays, but is not good for resumes. Instead of writing "Fluent not only in English, but also in Spanish," it's better to write "Fluent in English and Spanish."

TIP #47: Acronyms

Acronyms associated with a specific profession can play a helpful role **if** that term represents knowledge or skills which would be useful in your next job. Here are some guidelines:

- Acronyms are useful if they are generally understood in the profession. For example:

  Rhonda might have PIMS on her resume without explaining what it stands for, i.e. Profit Impact of Marketing Strategy. Since Rhonda plans to continue in the marketing profession, this acronym should be understood immediately by recruiters who will read her resume.

- Acronyms are **not** useful if they are used only in a specific firm or among a narrow group of people. In such cases, use a generic description or definition. For example:

  Lauren would not use the acronym TARYAG which was the in-house computer package used by a previous employer. No one outside the firm would have a clue as to what the acronym means. What Lauren should do is develop a generic term instead, for example, "Reduced turn around time for customer orders by 10% by introducing new uses for company's existing computer package."

In a related way, David would not use banking acronyms since banking is precisely the field he wishes to leave. For example, rather than referring to the ABA (American Bankers Association), David could say "Presented study on dilemmas in credit analysis to local chapter of professional association." Stating things this way, David also avoids confusing bankers with lawyers—American Bar Association (ABA).

Simply listing a string of acronyms is not to your best advantage. It is better to integrate these terms in resume sentences, with one acronym per sentence being the limit.

Let's return to Rhonda for an example. A sentence like this drowns the recruiter in acronyms: "Developed expertise in PIMS, IMD, MRD." A stronger approach would be this: "Reduced advertising costs through principles of PIMS. Expanded SMR training, resulting in a 10% gain in market share. Persuaded senior managers to simplify MRD, resulting in fewer shipment errors."

TIP #48: Useless Words

Some words are perfectly good in many situations, but not on resumes:

"Assisted"—Remember that your resume should tell your next employer about positive characteristics you can bring to the job. What does "assisted" say about you? Perhaps you sharpened pencils or arranged the conference chairs.

Think about what **you** demonstrated, achieved or learned that was of value. Rather than write: "Assisted in creation of new product," it is more informative to write:

"Researched potential price points for new product."

or

"Identified untapped market for gizmos, contributing to introduction of a new product line."

"**Responsible for…**"—This term helps you avoid the hard thought you may need to identify an appropriate action verb, but you are sacrificing impact. For example:

> "**Responsible for accurate and timely filing of monthly reports.**"

is weaker than

> "**Filed accurate monthly reports, often beating deadlines.**"

"Responsible for…" doesn't say that you did the job well or what you achieved. Besides, it is the language of a dry-as-dust job description, not a lively resume.

On a related point: When you say something about yourself (e.g. researched; identified) you are not implying that you were the only one who did so. There is no need to say "One of fifteen people who researched…". If you want to include the aspect of team work, write, "**Identified untapped market for gizmos as part of a six person team.**"

TIP #49: Use Modifiers Sparingly

Modifiers (e.g., adjectives and adverbs) can be marvelous when writing an essay, but use them sparingly when writing a resume. The reason is that extra words often muffle impact instead of enhancing it. Let's look first at some examples of adverbs:

> "**Cooperated *closely* and *effectively* with engineering team to design marketable gizmo.**"

By deleting the modifiers, Max came up with a more telegraphic sentence.

"Cooperated with engineering team to design marketable gizmo."

Modifiers in a resume context often add nothing to the significance of a sentence. After all, no one would write "worked remotely and ineffectively." The space you save by omitting modifiers helps make your resume appear less crowded. Alternately, you could use the space for something of greater value, like results. For example:

"Cooperated with engineers to design a marketable gizmo which increased revenue by 10%"

Adverbs can be particularly ill-advised at the beginning of a sentence:

WEAKER SENTENCE: Adverb at Beginning	MORE POWERFUL SENTENCE: Adverb deleted or deferred
Currently developing...	Developing...
Annually improved profitability...	Improved profitability annually...
Significantly improved...	Improved by 10%
Quickly established rapport...	Established rapport quickly

Adjectives, too, are often extraneous. For example, "Wrote *excellent* proposal..." Since no one would write "mediocre proposal," the word excellent doesn't add anything.

In addition, adjectives are usually less powerful than quantified results. For example, adding "which resulted in 8% cut in leasing cost" is far stronger than "excellent" or any adjective imaginable.

TIP #50: Always Use Positive Language

Your resume will be more appealing if you use positive terminology: Resume language which is half full is more powerful than language which is half empty. Here are some examples.

NEGATIVE TERMINOLOGY	POSITIVE TERMINOLOGY
■ Avoided disaster	■ Rescued
■ Threatened underachievers	■ Motivated staff
■ Only 1/3 of projects failed	■ Achieved 67% success rate
■ Limited revenue loss to 20%	■ Recognized 80% of original value
■ Developed chemical compound which didn't explode	■ Developed stable, non-exploding chemical compound

TIP #51: Be Succinct

Use one word instead of two where possible. Your resume will pack more punch if you use fewer words to convey any given thought. Review your resume to identify opportunities to replace two or three words with just one. Some common examples follow:

TOO VERBOSE	MORE EFFECTIVE
■ in regards to	■ regarding
■ as well as	■ and
■ in the course of	■ when
■ time to time	■ periodically
■ more than 50	■ 50

TIP #52: Avoid Repetition

In general, each experience should be used to convey a positive characteristic which has not already been presented. For example, Rhonda has done analytical work in each of her three jobs. In presenting her experience at Currentco, Rhonda mentioned her analytical skills. It is probably not necessary to repeat "analyzed" for Secondco and Firstco. An exception would be a situation where analytical skills were so central to the job that "analyzed" might bear repeating.

TIP #53: Naming Clients/Proprietary Information

Be careful that your resume doesn't reveal information contrary to the wishes of a current or past employer. The names of clients, sensitive product information or strategic plans are cases in point. The table below indicates a better approach in those situations.

	Inappropriate	Appropriate
client names	Designed publicity releases for Fantastic, Inc.	Designed publicity releases for a Fortune 50 consumer product company
product information	Identified XCL-30 genome as key to cloning a left handed golfer	Identified key genome in human cloning; **or:** researching genome for human cloning.

TIP #54: References

In most cases, listing the names of references on your resume serves no useful purpose. After all, nobody would list a negative reference, and most references you might list are not known to the recruiter. Generally an expression like "References available upon request" is sufficient and even this may be omitted if space is a problem.

However, in some instances indicating specific references can be an asset:

- **References are requested:** Two or three references would probably be sufficient unless a larger number is requested.

- **Overcoming suspicion:** Listing a current supervisor strongly suggests that you are not about to be fired for performance reasons. If you are about to be caught in a downsizing, this is something to consider.

- **Well known reference:** If the name of your reference is likely to be recognized and admired by the resume reader, include it. An example would be a person seeking a position in broadcast journalism and Tom Brokaw is willing to be a reference.

The name, title and phone number of each reference can be listed on a separate sheet of paper and appended to your resume in order to keep your main text to one page.

Warning: If you are listing someone as a reference, make sure to get that individual's permission first. Ask if s/he would be willing to provide a **favorable** reference for you if contacted by a prospective employer. You can help your reference help you by letting him/her know about the nature of the prospective position and the reasons for your interest in it. Obviously, be certain that asking for a reference doesn't jeopardize your current job.

In Chapter 6 we learned important tips for the "Experience" section of your resume. The next chapter will discuss your "Education" section.

7

Education

W here should you put "Education" on your resume? For individuals who have been working for at least several years, education will probably *follow* Experience on your resume. A recent college graduate will usually put Education *prior to* Experience since college education is likely to be your best selling point. Career changers, particularly those who recently acquired a degree closely related to their new career goal also will probably put Education first.

TIP #55: Making It More Than a Diploma

What should Education say about you? At a minimum, you should indicate the highest level of formal education you attained and the name of the institution which conferred your diploma.

For example, Gabrielle has two college degrees:

EDUCATION

Master of Science in Microbiology   June, 1997
University of Knowledge, Glenmark, CA

Bachelor of Science   May, 1993
University of Texas (El Paso)
Major: Biology

Gabrielle would put the higher degree (i.e., Master of Science) first.

David transferred from one college to another. He would mention first the institution which conferred his degree.

EDUCATION

Bachelor of Arts   May 1996
Carter College, Atlanta, GA
Major: Economics

Transferred from Fulton College (1994)

Education provides an opportunity to show positive characteristics beyond your diploma. The six Tips which follow give you some helpful examples.

TIP #56: Explain What You Gained

You may want to explain what you gained from your college experience. Here are a few examples of items you could note under Education:

- Curriculum emphasized analytical thinking, communication skills and team work.

- Major: Economics (12 credits in Accounting)

- Developed excellent technical and laboratory research skills.

TIP #57: Research

Gabrielle, our scientist, has a special interest in researching antidotes for Talking Horse Syndrome (THS). In college, Gabrielle did some research on neural inhibitors, a possible approach for treating THS. Since Gabrielle's research could have appeal to her next employer, she decided to include her research under Education like this:

EDUCATION
Master of Science: Microbiology
University of Knowledge, Glenmark, CA (1994)
Master Research Project:

The Influence of Enzymes on Neural Inhibitors—
Analyzed existing data on neural inhibitors. Designed experiments to identify possible enzymes for inhibiting dysfunctional neural transmissions.

Bachelor of Science: Microbiology (1990)
University of Texas - El Paso

Including her college research makes good sense for Gabrielle since her research is directly related to the kind of work she

would like to do in her next position. An additional possibility
is to write about research which indicates skills that are needed
for your next job, even if the *topic* of the research is not.
Research which is not related by topic or skills used should not
be included under Education, if at all.

TIP #58: Group Project

Larry is a forthcoming liberal arts graduate. His Education can
tell more about him than his academic interests alone. For example, ability to work well in groups, self reliance and strong
work ethic would be major attractions to employers. Therefore,
Larry's Education might be presented like this:

EDUCATION:
Mt. Herald College, South Hadley, MA
Bachelor of Arts, May, 1998
Major: Political Theory

**Worked 25 hours per week during academic
periods. Self-financed 90% of college living expenses.**

Group Projects:
- Researched student voter participation as part of four
  person team. Wrote detailed proposal for increasing
  overall political participation. Resulted in establishment
  of a polling district on campus and formation of student
  advocacy group on behalf of College.
- Designed questionnaire to identify major trends in student political thinking. Persuaded representative sample
  to devote time to giving extended responses. Conclusions reported in the daily campus newspaper.

Larry has placed the name of his college before the title of his degree because he believes that the prestige of this institution confers a benefit to him.

TIP #59: Study Abroad

Let's imagine for a moment that Larry had studied in Spain during his junior year. If Larry had wanted to draw attention to the fluency in Spanish he developed there, he might devote several lines to present that fact. For example:

EDUCATION:

Mt. Herald College, South Hadley, MA
Bachelor of Arts May 1998
Major: Political Theory

Study Abroad: University of Seville (Spain). Studied political and economic history in Spanish. Wrote paper in Spanish about Spain's post-Franco relationship with Europe.

On the other hand, if Larry's main point is simply that he has been abroad, he should allocate only one line:

University of Seville (Spain), Junior Year

TIP #60: Selective Honors

Awards for civic virtue or an outstanding accomplishment are an asset and should be mentioned. It is a good idea to indicate the reason the honor was conferred. For example:

Honors:

Alpha Beta Gamma Society—In recognition of outstanding contributions to campus historical preservation.

Einstein Memorial—Awarded to student who best exemplifies the Theory of Relativity in daily life.

TIP #61: Thinking About Grades

Since Rhonda graduated college years ago, the significance of her grades has diminished to the vanishing point. If her grades were excellent, such as **cum laude**, she could mention it but this would not be a major point influencing her probability of being interviewed for a job.

Grades **are** a factor for a recent graduate like Larry since they are correlated in people's minds with ability and/or seriousness of purpose. As a rule of thumb, a grade point average of 3.0 or better (where 4.0 = A) becomes something of a selling point. In Larry's case, his grades are good and he can present them plainly and quickly. For example:

Overall GPA = 3.2   Major GPA = 3.5

What about someone whose academic record is not very strong? Three of the common reasons for this situation can be addressed ethically and positively if they apply to you. First, your overall grades may have suffered when you were enrolled in a different program. Second, you had a particularly bad semester. You could indicate your GPA **except** for that unrepresentative circumstance as long as you clearly indicate what is being excluded. Third, you may have worked many hours per week to pay for your education. Your work ethic and self reliance may well overshadow some weakness in your grades.

This concept of "grades with an explanation" is not universally welcomed by recruiters. However, the recruiter who excludes you on this basis might exclude a recent graduate who indicates low grades or no grades. In any event, on balance, I recommend this approach when it accurately describes and explains the reasons for a less than stellar grade point average. Look at page 74 for an example of each case mentioned above.

In the last three chapters we learned about the Heading, Summary, and Experience sections of resumes. In Chapter 8 we will examine Other Selling Points (OSPs).

Examples of Grades With an Explanation

Example #1 (Transferred from another program):

Major GPA: 3.1
Overall GPA: 3.0 (since transferring from Engineering
Program as a sophomore)
> **or**

Major GPA: 3.1
Overall GPA: 2.8 (overall average suffered due to grades
while in Engineering Program)

Example #2: Particularly bad semester:
(Sometimes a special circumstance hurts your grades for a
limited period of time. You could explain this briefly.)

Major GPA: 3.2
Overall GPA: 3.0 (except for a poor freshman year)
> **or**

Major GPA: 3.2
Overall GPA: 2.7 (would be a 3.0 except for poor freshman year)

Example #3: Worked half-time or more:

Major GPA: 3.1
Overall GPA: 2.9 (Worked 30 hours a week every
academic semester to finance education.)

In a case like this, employers may be far more
influenced by your hard work than by your grades.

8

Other Selling Points

S o far we have examined tips for the Summary, Education and Experience sections of your resume. Let's take a look now at Other Selling Points (OSPs) which could be valuable in winning an interview. Most OSPs get placed in the latter portion of your resume, but there is no absolute rule governing such placement.

TIP #62: Citizenship

For many job seekers, information about their citizenship can be a selling point.

- Dual National: if you are a citizen of the United States in addition to another country, you could write:

> **Citizenship:** Dual National, United States and Holland

A person with citizenship from a country where Nextco does business brings an additional asset to the firm. In this case, a Dutch employer with facilities in the US might be especially interested in dual citizens.

Let's say you are a U.S. citizen or permanent resident but your resume reflects service in a foreign army or a degree from a foreign college. If an employer believes (perhaps subconsciously and without any malign intent) that you have a visa problem, you may miss some interview opportunities. Clarify the situation by indicating that you are in fact a US citizen or permanent resident. For example:

> **Citizenship**: Permanent Resident of the United States.

If you are neither a US citizenship nor a US Permanent resident, it is very difficult to be hired for a legal job in the United States. Although there is a theoretical possibility of being sponsored by a US employer, in practice this happens with relative infrequency.

TIP #63: Language Skills

Language skills are an asset. Languages open your eyes to other cultures and tend to broaden your horizons. Knowledge of a language can make you more comfortable in the presence of people whose first language is not English. This is a potential advantage for businesses with global customers or suppliers. What's more, many Americans have a culture which is immersed in another language. In short, knowledge of another language is never a negative; it's often an asset.

How should you treat languages on your resume?

- **Be honest about your degree of fluency.** For example: "Thoroughly bilingual, English and Spanish" implies that you could hold an intelligent conversion in either language. The ability to read a menu does not constitute fluency.

  "Conversant in French" implies that if you got lost on the Paris Metro, you could ask for directions and understand the response.

- **Specify reading, writing and speaking if** language is clearly important to the prospective employer. For example:

  "Fluent in reading and speaking Japanese. Moderate ability in writing."

- **Put languages in context or clarify to help the reader.** For example:

  "Fluent in two Chinese dialects (Mandarin/Cantonese)"
  "Fluent in Farsi (Persian)"

TIP #64: Travel

Sometimes travel adds a dimension to your life which could be valuable to an employer. Here are some examples:

- If you have never lived outside of your home state, you may use travel to show how you broadened your perspective.

> **Travel**: Backpacked through Midwest and deep South. Learned how to plan carefully, make prudent decisions and adjust to changing social norms.

- If your next job might include extensive contact with European clients and Americans who love to discuss their trips abroad, use travel to imply a comfort level with those clients.

> **Overseas Travel**: Lived in Paris for two months; traveled extensively throughout Western Europe.

- Lauren wanted to show that she hadn't always been a homebody, even though she had been away from the workforce for a number of years. Although she actually disliked the constant relocation caused by her father's military career, Lauren saw how she could now use that situation to her advantage, if a willingness to relocate might be important in her next job.

> **Geographic Mobility:** Willing to relocate to advance career. Lived in seven states and three countries (Germany, Philippines and Saudi Arabia) growing up in a military family.

Many people love to travel, but their vacation trips don't provide a reason to interview them. Don't include travel unless it presents a selling point.

TIP #65: Computer Skills

Computer skills are easily identified on your resume simply by listing them. For example

> **Computer Skills:** C++, Microsoft, Lotus Notes, Access

It makes sense to group programming languages first, followed by software packages for ease of reading. If your computer skills are a major selling point, you may want to delineate more explicitly. For example:

Languages: C++, COBOL
Software: Autocad, Excel, Access
Operating Systems: UNIX, OS/2, DOS, Windows '95

You probably will not need to articulate each part of MS Office or Coral Suite 8 unless you are looking for a position in data entry or word processing.

TIP #66: Professional Credentials

Professional credentials which pertain to your career goals are a definite selling point. Common examples are licenses and certifications. Here are some examples:

- IEUU
- Certified Financial Planner
- CLU

If the credential is commonly recognized, at least in your field, an acronym is sufficient. When in doubt, spell it out.

Related professional credentials are such a strong selling point that this topic deserves to be a category of its own:

Professional Certifications:
Certified Management Accountant (1995)
Certified Financial Analyst (1997)

Licenses and credentials unrelated to your career goals should be omitted.

TIP #67: Professional and Civic Honors

Recognition for professional accomplishments and the respect of your fellow citizens can be a selling point for two reasons. First, your respect and recognition can rub off on your employer. Second, they show a striving for excellence which enhances your own potential for advancement and provides an inspiration for other employees.

David wanted to present his honors to allay concern that he was leaving his current profession as a malcontent or an incompetent. He made sure to explain the basis for his honors for two reasons. First, outside of his current profession, people would not be familiar with the awards. Second, David wanted the awards to demonstrate generic characteristics valuable to his **next** employer and not narrow characteristics of specific importance only to his current profession.

> **Professional Awards:**
> Ofie Trophy: Awarded for exceptional creativity (1998)
> Hack Plaque: For outstanding use of computer innovations
>   (1996)

Let's assume for a moment that Gabrielle wanted to move into a managerial role within her technical profession. She was able to show team work and communication skills (in addition to her technical expertise) under Experience. Gabrielle's civic award would show the added dimension of leadership.

> **Civic Awards:**
>
> **Citizen of the Year** (1998), Winston-Salem, NC
> Award to the individual who best exhibits civic leadership
> **Soccer Mom of the Year** (1996), Winston-Salem, NC
> Award for leading the league in recognition from media and elected officials

TIP #68: Professional Associations

Membership in a professional association (e.g., Marketing Mavens of America) is an asset if:

- The Association is related to your *next* job

- You are active in the Association and wish to demonstrate the quality of leadership

- The Association could be a source of clients or customers for your next employer

If you are changing fields, listing current professional association memberships can be detrimental. For example, if you want to leave government social work to become a financial analyst, do not emphasize involvement with a non-profit, helping profession.

TIP #69: Military Service

Military service can be an excellent selling point, especially if you can present it in the right way. Let's look at a few examples:

Lauren continued to serve as a sergeant in the National Guard even after leaving the regular work force to raise her family. Her military experience could demonstrate several things:

- Leadership of both men and women

- Involvement outside the home

- Balance of family responsibility with a job (albeit part-time)

Lauren's presentation of her military experience might look like this:

Military Experience

Massachusetts National Guard—Ft. Devens. Platoon leader. Lead squad of 12 men and women in this mechanized unit. Train recruits. Plan logistic for full field maneuvers. Motivated squad to win special commendation in area-wide war games. Remaining military obligation is two weeks per year plus one weekend per month (1996-present)

Let's assume for the sake of our example that Larry had served in the army for three years prior to starting college. His military experience could show a sense of discipline and maturity which would not always be associated with his classmates. In addition, Larry can show that he has been outside his home state and met a diversity of people.

Military Experience

United States Army   (1992-1995)

Served on several infantry bases throughout the South and Southwest. Tour of duty under NATO in Germany. Molded squad of 12 men and women from diverse ethnic and class backgrounds into a cohesive combat-ready unit. Developed time-management and precision skills. Commended for exemplary conduct during war-game maneuvers.

If Larry had learned specific technical skills or had completed specific advanced training schools, he could mention it. Larry was neither an officer nor an NCO, so there would be no benefit in mentioning his rank.

TIP #70: Interests, Hobbies, Activities

Many people include a section regarding their interests, hobbies and/or activities. Consider the following points before including a section of this type.

- Since this section will probably not help you **get into** the interview, you may have better uses for this space.

- If you **are** invited to an interview, this section may generate a question or two designed for breaking the ice. Therefore be sure you are comfortable discussing what you wrote.

- **Never** add this section just to fill space. Imagine the following scene. You are asked at an interview "I see that you are interested in wrestling. What do you enjoy most?" If you respond, "Well, I used to wrestle in high school, now I mostly watch it on TV," you will be getting off to a weak start and may lose some credibility.

- Remember that an "activity" is something you are or were **active** in, not something you did casually once in a while.

Here are two examples from members of our Job Search Club:

Larry has decided to show his college activities, especially **team** sports to demonstrate involvement with others and student government to show **leadership**.

Activities: Play intramural rugby and basketball. Elected to Dorm Council three times and Student Senate twice.

Lauren may be entering a client centered business in which social sports are an asset. Therefore she might write:

Hobbies: Golf, tennis, gardening

Lauren might be tempted to play up her golf and tennis if she were applying to a company which makes balls for those sports, but that would be a mistake. A sporting goods manufacturer is looking for competent business and technical professionals. **Over-emphasizing** your sports hobby is likely to distract attention from what really counts: "Do you have the business or professional talents my company needs?"

TIP #71: Be Prudent

If you include religious or political involvements as an OSP, be careful not to be too specific in your identification.

- **Religious affiliation:** Religion should not be a factor in hiring, but unfortunately prejudice still exists. If you think your choir involvement will help you get interviewed, include it. However, it is better to write "Active in church choir" than to identify a specific denomination.

- **Political involvement:** If political experience or connections would be an asset, you may want to include this. Similarly, your involvement may be an opportunity to show public speaking or organizing skills. However, you are best advised not to identify a specific candidate or party, unless you are trying to get a position with a specific politician or political party.

9

Dealing With Dates

TIP #72: Dates—When They Are an Asset

Sometimes dates can be an asset. For example, let's say you have made good progress within your current or most recent place of employment. The dates for each job within the firm could be included to draw attention to your upward development. Jannine is a case in point. As noted in the sample below, Jannine has been with Quality, Inc. for fifteen years. To show that she hasn't been stuck in the mud there, Jannine could show the four different positions she has had at Quality, Inc. with their corresponding dates. In that way, Jannine is showing professional progress. Notice that Jannine does not indicate in a single date her fifteen years with the same employer because that fact **per se** would not be an asset.

Quality, Inc., Omaha, NB

Vice President for Research (1993-present)

Manager of Product Development (1988-1993)

Project Director (1984-1988)

Research Associate (1982-1984)

To achieve a similar goal, Jannine could decide to discuss only her most recent, and presumably highest level, position. In that case, Jannine would deal with previous positions simply by showing a title and date, as shown below:

QUALITY, INC. Omaha, NB

Vice President for Research (1993 - present)

Previously served as:
Research Manager (1988 - 1993)
Project Director (1984 - 1988)
Research Associate (1982 - 1984)

Sheila has worked for three employers in the same industry over the last ten years and has decided to organize her work experience by industry. Since Sheila believes that her industry experience is an asset, she can state the length of her industry experience explicitly and prominently. For example:

PROFESSIONAL EXPERIENCE

Electronics Industry (1986 - present)

Widget Co._____

_____

_____

_____ (1993 - present)

Gadget, Inc._____

_____

_____

_____ (1988 - 1993)

Electrogize, Inc._____

_____

_____

_____ (1986 - 1988)

TIP #73: When Dates Are Not an Asset

Your resume should indicate the dates of employment for the work experience you discuss. How **prominent** you make the dates is a matter of choice, however.

In many cases, it is best to position a date so that it will be a fact but not a factor. That is, since a date will seldom help you, make it as neutral as possible. One good way to do this is to position your dates **at the end** of the text related to that experience. For example:

Gadgetco Limited, Walrun Grove, CA

Market Analyst
Investigated possible market niches for a newly invented robotic broom. Analyzed data bases to determine high-probability SKU's. Surveyed potential users to identify concerns. Recommended a modified design which became a category leader (1995-1997).

This approach is useful in two cases. First, utilizing a neutral, less prominent location helps minimize the visibility of potential knockouts such as gaps in employment (e.g., "too long" in one position, or, "too brief" a time in one position). The potentially troublesome dates will still be sought by the recruiter, but the more favorable aspects of your resume are likely to be considered as well. Second, your dates may be less prominent if other considerations like space or aesthetic appearance are more important.

TIP #74: Dates and Diplomas

The date of your college graduation is an asset if it is very recent or forthcoming shortly. The newness of your diploma fits nicely with entry level situations and also explains why you have little, if any, professional experience.

On the other hand, if your graduation date is not recent you have nothing to gain by including it. On the contrary you might have something **to lose** if the date indicates gaps in your employment or slow **progress** in your field. In some cases, your graduation date may trigger negative perceptions, albeit illegal ones, in regard to age. In general, unless you have graduated college recently, **do not** indicate your graduation date.

10

Editing, Exceptions, and Interview Preparation

TIP #75: Editing Your Resume

Gabrielle finished the last line of her resume and put down her pen with great satisfaction. (Many other people write directly with a word processor; then print out their handiwork). "At last I am finished" Gabrielle proclaimed with relief. "On second thought, maybe, I'm not finished yet," she reflected. Gabrielle wrote a checklist of items to review:

- **Space Allocation:** Did you allocate the most space to your most important selling points? If not, consider reallocating ½ inch or 1 inch of space in favor of your more important point.

- **Repetition:** You may have repeated sentences starting with the same action verb. If the positive characteristic you want to display is very important, that makes sense. If not, either **delete** one or more sentences, use **synonyms** for the action verb, or **restructure** one sentence to present a different positive characteristic.

- **Length:** In Tip #38, we talked about deciding between a one or two page resume. One way to control the length of your resume is this:

  Identify the five most important lines in your draft. Then the next five and so on. When you reach the third or fourth batch of five lines, there is a good chance some of that material can be removed from your resume.

- **Format:** Gabrielle looked at her main categories to make sure they were logically presented and consistent with the points she wanted to make.

- **Positive Characteristics:** Gabrielle made sure that her resume explicitly indicated the skills and characteristics her next employer would want and Gabrielle could offer.

- **Avoiding Knockouts:** Gabrielle was alert for material on her resume which might work against her.

- **Neatness:** Did her resume look like something a recruiter would find pleasant to read?

TIP #76: A Two Part Litmus Test

Every statement on your draft resume should pass a two part litmus test:

- **Will the statement help me gain a job interview**? There is a lot you could say about yourself. If a statement will help you be invited to an interview, include it. If not, why include it?

- **Is every statement true:** This means clearly and un-equivocally. A statement which needs a lawyer to defend it fails the litmus test.

Re-read your resume to make sure it passes both parts of this litmus test.

TIP #77: Exceptions to the One Page Rule of Thumb

This book advocates a one page resume for workers without a great deal of experience, with two pages being reasonable for more experienced workers. However, there are times to relax these restraints. Let's take a look:

Electronic Submission

If you are submitting an electronic resume (e-mail or by template) to a database, page limitation is not a major factor. First, the initial "reading" will be done by a machine which won't care about your resume's length. Second, a longer resume could provide the opportunity for more "hits" when the database is searched in response to a hiring requisition.

If you are comfortable with your personal computer, you may

wish to submit your regular resume to the database. You could insert the disk which contains your paper resume's text, download it to the database using a "cut and paste" technique. The advantages of doing this are speed and accuracy—using a text you have already reviewed and proofread. The disadvantage is that the editing tools on the receiving end (e.g., for formatting) may be difficult to use.

For more about electronic resumes, see Joyce Lain Kennedy's *Electronic Resume Revolution* (John Wiley) and Pete Weddle's *Internet Resumes* (Impact Publications).

Remember: Writing a longer resume should not be an occasion for poor organization or extraneous information.

Secondary Information

A second page may be in order to indicate employment of value, but of less than compelling interest. Some people put only good news on page one and possible drawbacks on page 2. A second page may also be in order for secondary information such as publications or presentations. Other examples are skills which are nice to have, but not critical to the specific job. Examples might be languages and computer skills in cases where these are not of primary interest to the employer.

TIP #78: Bolding For Clarity

With most word processors it is easy to make a word or phrase stand out by **bolding**. You can use bolding constructively for these purposes:

- **Logic:** To show the logical construction of your resume, bold the main categories (e.g., Summary, Experience, Education, Computer Skills).

- **Attention**: To draw attention to the better selling point when two are closely situated. For example, bold your job title **or** the name of your employer depending on which would be more attractive to a recruiter. Similarly, you may want to draw attention to a particularly critical part, such as "Permanent Resident of the United States" or licenses and certificates which are essential for your next job.

Tip #79: Tailoring Your Resume

Let's say that you have written a terrific resume, including a thorough edit. You may still wish to **tailor** your resume. "Tailoring" in our context means altering a resume's format or content to address the specific needs of a new job opportunity. Consider tailoring your resume to:

- Emphasize different positive characteristics to match the specific needs of a different kind of job.

- Emphasize or de-emphasize (depending on circumstances) an industry affiliation.

- Add or highlight those characteristics expressly requested in a help wanted notice.

- Reflect information about a specific job opportunity gathered from an information interview or similar source.

The inventory of positive characteristics you developed even before you started writing your resume is a good source of ideas for your tailored resume.

There are several examples of tailored resumes in Chapter 12.

A word to the wise: Don't leave it to your cover letter

Some people are concerned about the time and energy needed to tailor a resume to address different opportunities. Similarly some people correctly point to cover letters as an important tool in this regard. In fact, **we have included an entire chapter on this subject**. However, it would be a mistake to depend *solely* on the cover letter to tailor, the fit between your credentials and the employer's specifications. There are two reasons:

- **There may be no cover letter.**

   An example would be a **job fair** sponsored by a specific firm or designed for a specific profession. The identity of the sponsor is an invitation to tailor your resume accordingly, but there is no cover letter involved (See Tip #86). Similarly, you may be at an **informational meeting** with someone who could help you. On the chance that your resume will be requested, you could anticipate specific needs and tailor your resume accordingly. However, a cover letter will not be requested at an informational meeting. (See Tip #22)

- **Your cover letter may not be read.**

   It could become separated, or be ignored as a matter of practice. If an OCR is used, the cover letter is not always scanned. (See Tip #80)

TIP #80: A Scannable Resume

At the present time, most resumes are still read by a real human being who determines whether or not to invite the applicant to an interview. Sometimes, especially for high-tech positions, such as computer professionals and engineers, "reading" resumes is done by scanning them through a Optical Character Reader (OCR). This is especially true for resumes submitted for a high-tech position with a large employer. Therefore, it pays to consider the following to make your resume scannable.

- Do not use italics or underlines. Bolding can also present problems.

- Use asterisks (*) instead of bullets (•). OCR's may read a bullet as a period.

The absence of italics, underlines and bolding tends to make the resume less appealing to human eyes. Therefore, the changes you might make for the sake of scanning come at a price. I would make these changes only if:

- You know as a fact that your resume will be scanned.

- You are in a high-tech profession, e.g., computers or engineering, where scanning is very common.

TIP #81: Resume By E-mail

Let's take the situation when you identify a job lead using the Internet (See Tips #87-91). Individuals interested in applying may be requested to forward a resume by e-mail, or at least be given the option to do so. E-mail may mean free choice as to text or it may require utilizing the recruiter's template.

Free Choice

- **Prepare ahead:** Your paper resume has been carefully written, edited and proofread. Copy your resume on your e-mail, print it out and check it. Then it will be available whenever needed.

- **Title:** E-mail calls for a subject or title. The theme you developed in Tip #25 would be a good title. You may need to modify the theme since e-mail may impose a space restriction (e.g., 45 to 50 characters).

- **Graphics:** Graphic techniques like boxes can be problematic for e-mail. You are better advised to avoid them.

- **A Note of Caution on Attachments**: It is best to import the text file of your resume into the message you are sending itself. Avoid sending a file attachment, and don't send your resume as a word processing attachment. Many employers will not open the attachment.

Template

- Follow the prompt and instructions. Unfortunately this restricts your creativity and may force you into a resume style, let's say chronological, which is not your preference.

- When you see a colon (:), leave a space before entering text.

Stick to the text of your paper resume as much as possible. This will save you from giving spontaneous responses you haven't considered well or redrafting your resume for every template.

TIP #82: A Blue Collar Resume

The members of our Job Search Clubs we follow in this book are all seeking white collar jobs. However, there are millions of good blue collar jobs and the tips in this book are generally applicable in those cases as well. A few modifications are in order:

Education

- If you didn't graduate from a college, name your **high school** and the town and state of its location.

- List the **certificates** you earned which indicate a specific skill.

Experience

- Who you are may show best through what you do. The tasks you perform and the specific machines you use are more likely to be good selling points than for your white collar neighbor.

TIP #83: When Your Resume Is Not For a New Job

Sometimes you will need a resume that is **not** written with a new job in mind. Here are some situations to consider:

- **Company record:** Sometime your employer will request an updated resume for their file. Obviously, you *don't want* to include a Summary which indicates an interest in another job. However, you do want:

1. A **Summary** of your skills

2. An **Education** section which might include seminars attended on the firm's behalf and course work taken in the evening that would help you do your job better.

3. An **Experience** section which includes accomplishments and positive comments from your annual performance review, if applicable.

4. To include company specific jargon.

- **Your Next Job:** After you have been at the job 3-6 months, start writing a resume with your next job in mind. Of course, your current accomplishments are important. However, you should also consider what positive characteristics you would want on your resume a year or five years from now. Then try to create opportunities to develop or demonstrate those characteristics if you don't already have them. Start to write your next job resume whether you plan to remain with your present employer or anticipate looking elsewhere.

A Graduate School Application

Many graduate schools prefer, or even require, full-time work experience as one criterion for admission. In that case:

- Your **Summary Statement** should indicate a connection between the graduate program and your career goals. For example "...Seeks to enter a top graduate program in preparation for a career as a product manager."

- Your **Education** should show adequate preparation through course work, important skills developed and a high level of academic success. For example, if you are applying to a graduate program in economics:

Bachelors of Arts 1995
Nicepalms University, Boca Raton, FL

Major: Economics   Minor: Statistics

Overall GPA 3.5   Major GPA 3.4

- Your **Experience** should show work ethic, insights about a related field and/or skills developed.

- Your **Other Selling Points** should include helpful tools, like computer packages used in the field you hope to enter.

Resume as Interview Preparation

The primary purpose of your resume is to get you into the interview room in an honest way. Your resume can also help you prepare to interview better. Let's look at the following tips and see how:

Tip #84: Learning More About Yourself: Asking How and Why

Your job interview will explore the potential match between you and what a specific employer requires. The better the match, the better your chances of receiving a job offer.

As part of your interview preparation, have a friend ask you "how" and "why" about each line of your resume. There are two reasons. First, your interviewer may well ask some "how" or "why" questions, so your practice may have a direct application. Second, many people think about themselves in terms of "what" and "when." Thinking about "how" and "why" will help you see yourself in a more complete light. Look at Tip #85. A friend could help Lauren by asking:

"How did you manage to raise $250,000?"

"Why did you organize concert tours for your at risk children?"

TIP #85: Test Flight: Friends and Strangers

Is your resume delivering the message you intended? Before sending it to a prospective employer, ask at least one friend and one comparative stranger for a few moments of assistance.

- **Friends:** Ask one or more friends to read your resume quickly. Then ask him/her two questions "Based on my resume how would you describe me?" and "Do you think this resume *accurately* describes me?"

- **Strangers:** Show your resume to someone you don't know well. Perhaps someone who is a friend of a friend. Ask him/her to describe you in a few words based on your resume.

If both friends and strangers perceive you as you intended, the content of your resume is probably well presented. If not, some changes may be in order.

An important bonus from Tip #84: You may gain some

additional ideas that you could incorporate into a revised version of your resume. For example, in answering the first question in Tip #84, Lauren might identify *researching* foundations as an important component of raising $250,000. *Research* could then be added to her resume.

11

Outreach

In the previous Tips, we learned how to write a dynamite resume. Now it is time to explore ways to put your resume in front of a prospective employer.

TIP #86: Make Good Use of Job Fairs

Picture a shopping mall. One of its features is that it contains many stores under one roof. If one or more of these stores turn out to be of interest, a visit to the mall can be rewarding.

A job fair has some of the characteristics of a mall. Many companies will have a booth of some type and a representative present to speak with people who come by. The company's goal is two fold: one, to attract applicants it might otherwise miss; two, to identify people to invite for an interview. In respect to the second point, the job fair **is not** like a mall. If you are just casually shopping around, you are less likely to be considered a good candidate for a job interview. Here's what you should do:

- **Dress professionally.** This means a business suit for both men and women.

- **Speak with the employer representative.** Don't just drop your resume on the table and walk away. Ask some thoughtful questions about the firm and possible career opportunities for you. If there is a potential match leave your resume and ask for the representative's business card. Give the representative a firm handshake and take a company brochure for reference. Hint: Don't overstay your welcome. Spending more than five minutes with any single representative will leave a negative impression if others are waiting to speak with him/her. You might say "I appreciate speaking with you, but I see that others are waiting. Is there a convenient time when we could continue our conversation?"

- **Follow-up with a brief letter.** A follow-up letter increases your chance for being offered an interview at some point in the future because it demonstrates above average motivation. In addition, follow through is, in itself, recognized by employers as a positive professional characteristic. A sample letter appears on page 105.

Here are some ways you can find out about job fairs which may be of interest to you:

- Examine several sites on the Internet which announce job fairs. For example:

Career Expo Job Fairs: *http://www.careerex.com*
Career Mosaic: *http://www.careermosaic.com*

1324 Jerome Road
Menlo Park, CA 94025

June 10, 1998

Ms. Jennifer Brownley
Project Manager
Amazing Disk Drive, Inc.
9210 Spruce Street
Irvine, CA 92718

Dear Ms. Brownley,

It was a pleasure meeting you at the Extremely Hi-Tech Job Fair in Irvine yesterday. I enjoyed our conversation about Amazing Disk Drive and career possibilities for people trained in computer information systems.

Following our discussion, I read the literature you gave me about ADD's products and recent performance. I was impressed and would like to discuss job opportunities for me with ADD in a quieter environment than a job fair can provide.

Next week, I will call you to see if a meeting can be arranged. Another copy of my resume is enclosed for your convenience.

Sincerely yours,

Irene Nakosteen

Irene Nakosteen
Enclosure

There are even real time actual job fairs held in Cyber Space. For example, Cyber Fair (TM) on HEART, at

http://www.career.com

- Read the trade publications of your **next** profession. Fairs advertised there are likely to be highly correlated with your interests. Also, check with the regional trade associations of relevance to you:

- Check with your local Chamber of Commerce.

- Check the business and help wanted sections of your local and regional newspapers for job fair announcements.

Use the Net

The Internet provides additional means of access to employers. A potential advantage is that you can now identify employers from your home computer or public library (if it is connected to the Internet). A potential disadvantage is that you will neglect more traditional avenues. Remember, the Internet is an added tool, not a magic pill. Finding a good job is not like ordering merchandise from a catalogue.

TIP #87: Use the Bulletin Boards

There are a number of Web sites which post job opportunities. These are often called bulletin boards. Let's follow some of our Job Search Club members as they uncover and utilize appropriate bulletin boards.

Larry knows from his college placement office that the National Association of Colleges and Employers (NACE) has a bulletin board as part of its home page. Since he is a recent college graduate, it makes sense to start with a bulletin board expressly designed for his situation. Larry connected to the Web simply by clicking on the icon of his net server. He entered the URL for NACE's homepage (*http://www. jobweb.org*). "The URL is like the address for an apartment building. Each door in the building is marked and I can knock just on those of most interest to me," Larry noted. Just as an apartment building has many doors, a typical homepage may have many links. Larry moved his cursor to the icon marked "Jobs" and double clicked.

The next page Larry saw was marked "Jobs and Career Opportunities." "I will check the job postings first," Larry decided, "and check the employer directory later." Larry entered the word "marketing" in the narrow "query box," and scrolled down the page a bit. The next decision for Larry was whether to limit his job search geographically. Larry decided to enter "TX" for Texas since he planned to settle in the Lone Star State. In a matter of minutes, the bulletin board posted three job descriptions. One required an MBA, which Larry didn't have, the second was in San Antonio, which was not a good location for him and the third was a marketing representative in Houston with Maybeco. "The listing for Maybeco sounds interesting to me and the geography is right. This is a good lead to pursue," Larry said. In this case, the firm listed a mailing address as the contact information and Larry made a note of it. "This is really a lot like responding to a newspaper advertisement," Larry observed. "I will send a copy of my paper resume and an appropriate cover letter."

Larry also read Tips #81 and #92 to help him determine the best method for sending his resume: regular mail, fax, or e-mail.

A good reference book for exploring job search bulletin boards is *CareerXroads* by Gerry Crispin and Mark Mehler (MMC Group).

SOME USEFUL JOB SEARCH BULLETIN BOARDS AND LINKS*

America's Job Bank   *www.ajb.dni.us*
Career Path   *www.careerpath.com*
E-Span   *www.espan.com*
Job Trak   *www.jobtrak.com*
Monster Board   *www.monster.com*
Online Career Center   *www.occ.com*

*These Bulletin Boards and links are provided for the sake of example. You can find many more by utilizing a search engine (see below). Also the URL (net address) sometimes changes over time.

TIP #88: Using a Search Engine, Even When You Are Clueless

Lauren wasn't familiar with a specific URL (Homepage address) she could use. Therefore, she decided to utilize the "search engine" feature of the Web. Search engines are handy research tools which help you locate resources of value if you identify a specific topic. Lauren's local library was connected to the Web through Netscape and subscribed to several search engines.

Lauren chose Infoseek as her search engine. She could have chosen Magellan, Yahoo, or any of several others.

On the first screen there were a number of topics she could pursue in addition to a query box. Since "Find a Job" was one of the topics, she moved her cursor under those words and double clicked (other search engines will have helpful quiz boxes which may have different names). The next screen also contained several categories in addition to hypertext identification of ten potentially useful Web sites. In this case, there was a category called "Job Listing" so Lauren double clicked on it. "It makes sense to refine my search if I can before scrolling down on the screen," she noted.

The next screen identified a number of job listing topics. "If I knew that I wanted health care or high tech, I could double-click on that specific topic," Lauren noted. "However, at this point, I am not that specific in my search. I think it's time to scroll down to the titles of the web sites," she concluded.

Lauren found a number of possible leads to pursue including general bulletin boards and those based on geography and industry. At this point, Lauren followed the same process as Larry in Tip #87.

TIP #89: Using a Prospective Employer's Home Page

Many firms today have a home page on the Web. It is a convenient way to present potential customers and investors with important information about the company. In many cases, the company also provides information about employment opportunities.

Lauren discovered three quick ways to identify a company's home page address:

- Call the company's main telephone number and ask for their home page address. Sometimes this simple approach yields the fastest result.

- The missing piece of URL is what comes between "*www.*" and the last dot plus three characters ("*.com*" for commercial sites; "*.edu*" for educational sites; "*.org*" for any organization; and "*.gov*" for government agencies). Frequently the missing piece is simply the company's or organization's name. For example, the URL for the company **EDS** is simply *http://www.eds.com.*

- Enter the company's name in the query box of a search engine (Tip #88). If the company has a URL, you will probably see it on the first screen to appear.

Once you have connected to a firm's home page, look for a link which says something like "Employment Opportunities" or "Careers at (name of company)" and double click. Determine if you are interested in any of the opportunities indicated, and if so, how the company suggests you respond. If conventional mail is called for, your paper resume (accompanied by a cover letter) is appropriate. For e-mail resumes, see Tip #81.

TIP #90: Think Broadly: Using Links

In the previous two tips, Lauren used a search engine. One benefit of this approach is uncovering links to other sources which may be of interest to you. For example, lets take a hypothetical company and call it Flashco, a maker of flashing lights for railroad crossings. The same screen which identifies Flashco may identify URL's for related topics such as Flashco's competitors, railroads and major manufacturers of lights.

TIP #91: Search Newspaper Ads Electronically

Not all jobs are advertised in newspapers. In fact, some experts say that a majority are not advertised publicly at all. Even if this perception is accurate, thousands of jobs **are** advertised in newspapers every week. Why not take advantage of this resource?

It is possible to access newspaper help wanted ads on the internet. One good place to start is ***http://www.careerpath.com***. Let's follow David as he accesses ads in three different cities.

David accessed the Net using Netscape and entered the URL for Career Path given above. The Career Path home page appeared, including four separate icons. David doubled clicked on the word "Jobs" in order to search the help wanted database by newspaper, job category and keyword. A list of twenty-five major newspapers appeared. The instructions asked David to "Select at least one newspaper to search." David selected The Cincinnati Inquirer Post and the Columbus Dispatch because he was most interested in Ohio as a place to work. Then David used the scroll bar to select at least one job category. David chose three: Advertising, Customer Service and Education. For the third step, David entered two keywords (e.g., writing, communication) to narrow his search. Next, David chose "Display All Ads" as his display option and selected the most current week as the one he wanted to search. In this case, one of the papers had no matches for David, but the other had twelve under "Education." David double clicked on that word, and full length ads appeared on the next screen. One for a "list marketing specialist" and a second for a "development officer" in a college appealed to David. Each asked David to respond by mail, providing the appropriate address.

"I have identified two possibilities I might have missed otherwise," David said to himself. "Since I have read Tip #81 and Tip #92, I could have responded by e-mail or fax if that's what the prospective employer requested."

TIP #92: Faxing Your Resume

Here are some guidelines to consider when you think about faxing your resume:

- **Do** fax your resume if the recruiter specifically requests this means of response to a position which appears on an electronic bulletin board or in a newspaper help wanted notice.

- **Do** fax your resume if a friend calls with a hot job lead and requests a copy of your resume *immediately*.

Faxed copies tend to look less professional than paper copies. Faxes may also pose problems for OCR's. Therefore:

- **Don't** fax your resume when there is an alternative (e.g., paper or electronic resume).

- **Don't** fax your resume simply to use all resume delivery means known to mankind. If the same recruiter receives your resume through multiple modalities, his/her attitude towards you is liable to suffer.

TIP #93: Continue to Utilize Conventional Sources

Remember that computer resources are an additional tool, not the only tool to use. Conventional, non-computer sources are still valuable. Let's look at a few of them.

- **Chambers of Commerce:** Most communities have a local chamber of commerce which fosters business interests in that area. A chamber is a great place to obtain a list of local employers. Often such a list even indicates size and industry of the employer. Thus, a microbiologist could ferret out the names of potential employers by seeking firms of twenty (20) or more employees which might be doing work in microbiology. Another individual might use the list to prod their thinking about a potential next industry.

- **Local Press:** The local press often carries stories about new, expanding or significant companies, top 100 companies in some category, etc. A useful approach is to send your resume to a person mentioned in the press article. Your accompanying cover letter should make immediate reference to the article. For example:

1776 Heritage Drive
Jenkintown, PA 19075

March 25, 1998

Mr. Harry Fine
Director of Marketing
Incongruous Products, Inc.
1643 Central Ave.
Haventown, PA 19067

Dear Mr. Fine

The story in Today's Haventown Herald about Incongruous Products, Inc. was really impressive. I was especially struck by your statement that growth in the sale of ice cubes to Arctic Circle residents has been phenomenal.

My own professional experience includes marketing products to seemingly incongruous customers. For example, I established an outlet for snow shovels in Key West, Florida and a mail order business in beef patties for vegetarians. The annual revenue is $1.5 million and $24 million respectively.

Perhaps we could discuss a marketing role for me at Incongruous Products, Inc. My resume is enclosed. I will call you next week to see when a meeting can be arranged.

Sincerely,

Celia Ginzi-Bird

Celia Ginzi-Bird
Enclosure

Note: The details of this letter (e.g. ice cubes, snow shovels, beef patties) are obviously intended to add a light moment to your reading of this chapter. The actual examples in your letter would not be as improbable as these.

- **Help Wanted Ads:** A conventional adage holds that most job openings are not advertised. However, many jobs **are** advertised so don't overlook them.

Standard References

Standard references may be helpful in identifying potential employers. Examples include:

The Million Dollar Directory (Standard & Poors)
Hoover's Handbook of American Business (Hoovers)

TIP #94: Build and Use Your Human Networks

Human beings remain a prime asset in your job search. People are a great source of information about industries, companies and what a specific job is really like. Sometimes, people can even identify job leads for you. How do you access people who could be helpful, at least on an informational basis?

Lauren shared her experiences with us. She had been out of the workforce for a number of years, so she didn't have any direct connections in the field she was exploring, namely mutual funds. She identified three categories of people who could be helpful.

- **Warm calls:** Family members, friends and neighbors, all of whom would be glad to hear from her.

- **Tepid calls:** Friends of family members, neighbors of friends and other permutations of warm calls.

- **Cold calls:** People in the industry who were complete strangers.

Lauren approached her warm calls and asked each person if s/he had friends, neighbors, family or professional associates in the mutual funds industry. One neighbor's tennis partner was a broker-dealer named George who often advised clients about mutual funds. The neighbor asked George if Lauren could contact him and George agreed.

Lauren's questions to George helped her learn a great deal about mutual funds from a broker-dealer and client perspective. "I have gained practical insights I wouldn't pick up from a newspaper or a book," Lauren realized. Lauren also asked George if he could suggest a few names of people in mutual funds companies. Lauren assured George that she would pursue informational meetings, and not ask George's contacts for a job. George was so impressed by Lauren's preparation and professional demeanor, that he agreed. "In fact," George added, "Sally Forth at Mutual Money mentioned over lunch that she was looking for a good client communication person. Why don't you contact Sally and be sure to mention my name."

Receiving more than she had asked for, Lauren mailed Sally a cover letter and resume right away. At the same time, she sent a brief note to the other names (Ishwar and Janice) George had supplied. Because she was seeking **information** from these two individuals, Lauren did not include a resume. As it turned out, Lauren succeeded very quickly in arranging an informational meeting with Janice which gave Lauren a deeper understanding of mutual funds. By the time, she had a formal job interview with Sally two weeks later, Lauren had enough information to present herself as a competent individual who understood client communication and the demands of the mutual fund industry.

David asked about other ways of identifying prospects for information interviews. "For example, I am considering mall management, but I don't know anybody in that field," he said.

Rhonda suggested that David explore his local mall. "I bet they have a manager's office right there. Why not inquire about the manager's name and title. Then request a meeting." David sent a brief letter like the one below before calling with his request:

1776 Heritage Drive
Philadelphia, PA 19102

May 10, 1998

Mr. Vernon Rapp
Director of Mall Resources
Albion Property Management
76 Bells Corner
Philadelphia, PA 19152

Dear Mr. Rapp:

I am in the process of exploring a change in career. Mall management is a field I have identified and I would appreciate your insights and suggestions about the pragmatic issues involved with this career. Could you spend 15-20 minutes with me to discuss this industry?

Let me give you some personal background. For nine years I have worked in transportation logistics. Although I remain well employed, I am seeking other avenues for my talents. A recent article in *Retail Management* magazine attracted my interest in mall management as a possible next step.

Your time is precious and I promise to respect it. I will call you next week in the hope that you can offer me the benefit of your advice.

Sincerely,

David Goodman

David Goodman

Larry joined the discussion and raised a logical point "What kind of questions could you ask at an information interview," she inquired. Gabrielle had some recent experience in this area and shared questions she had asked when she sought information from a pharmaceutical researcher she interviewed for information. Gabrielle's questions may be a source of ideas for you.

GABRIELLE'S INFORMATION INTERVIEW QUESTIONS

1. What makes this position important to your firm?

2. Do you tend to work individually or in teams? Are the teams comprised of people from the same disciplines or from different fields?

3. How did you break into this field? Would your experiences still be typical today?

4. Is there a predictable seasonally to your work? What did you find stressful in your job? If there is such a thing as a typical day or week, could you please describe it?

5. How much of your work time is spent in primary research and how much is spent researching journals or attending meetings?

6. What other functions would you typically work with in the course of a week? For example, do you stay in close touch with the marketing and finance people?

7. What technical skills would I need to have to start in a field like this and what new skills would I develop over the course of time? What personal attributes does it take to succeed?

8. Do you belong to any professional societies? Would a nonmember be able to attend a meeting? What professional journals do you read regularly?

9. No one knows what the future will bring, but how do you think this profession may evolve over the next ten years or so?

10. If your son or daughter expressed a desire to go into this field, what would you say to him/her?

The notes you make at and after these information interviews will help you build your inventory of positive characteristics. That is a double win. A good inventory helps you write a better resume (see Tip #18) and answer questions better at a job interview.

TIP # 95: Send Your Resume to a Specific Individual

If you are sending your resume by regular mail or by fax, try to address a specific individual to receive your resume. Here are some ways to identify the best person.

- **Cold Calls:** Call a firm of particular interest to you and say "I have some correspondence for your marketing manager. Please give me that person's full name and proper title" (Make sure to check for the spelling of both the first and last names).

- **Professional Associations:** Most professional associations have a membership directory indicating names, titles and places of employment. Typical dues are $50 - $75 annually. Joining a professional association is a good idea in any event. Meetings may provide important contacts if you introduce yourself to people and membership itself makes your efforts more credible.

- **College Alumni:** Some colleges will provide you the name of a fellow alum if you ask like this, "I am an alum of Emeritus College, Class of 1992. Do we have any alumnus at Goodfellow Corp? I am particularly interested in someone in the information technology area."

- **Networking Names:** In the course of your informational interviewing you may have uncovered the names of people in your field of interest (See Tip #94).

In general, you are best advised to address correspondence to the individual with the highest title in your functional area. Examples would be Vice President - Research, District Manager, Controller. Even if your letter is referred to personnel, you have lost nothing by starting with the relevant top person. His/her routing slip on your resume may gain it a bit of extra attention.

TIP #96: Follow Through

A great resume and outreach plan are critical to your success in winning interviews, but there is also another step: follow-through. This is what you can do:

- Make a chart like the one below so you can track the outcome for each resume you submit.

Name of firm	Contact Person (Title)	Phone Number	Action to Date	Next Step
Wonderful company	Harry Stone (Director of Finance	(413) 976-1881	(April 1) left message on machine	Call again on April 9
Fantastico	Celia Goodman (Treasurer)	(617) 549-1987	(April 1) told resume referred to HR Department	Call HR on April 9 - ask who might have my resume
Dry, Inc.	Ellen Wettly (President)	(508) 876-1396	March 31 - E.W. out of town. Reads mail upon return	Short note to thank secretary - call E.W. on April 10
Hopeful & Hightime	Janice Dagi-Ellis (Finance Mgr.)	(413) 652-6521	Telephone interview scheduled for April 8 at 10:00 A.M.	Prepare for 30-60 minute interview

- One week after you mail a resume, call the individual to whom it was sent. You could say:

"This is Alba Goodpastor. I am checking up on a resume I sent last week. I would like to make sure that you received it and whether you need any additional information from me. Can you tell me anything about my status?"

- If you receive no informative response, call again 7 to 10 days later.

Your call is likely to be answered by a machine or a secretary who will simply take a message. That's all right. Calling can be a point in your favor. However, heed the warning below.

Warning: Do not make a pest of yourself. Calling more frequently than every 7 to 10 days makes you a nuisance, not an interview candidate. If you receive a response which indicates that further inquiries are not welcome, say "Thank you. I hope to hear from you when you have made a decision." If you are responding to a help wanted notice which says "no phone calls," honor that request.

TIP #97: When the Recruiter You Call Answers the Phone

Imagine that Lauren calls Jill, a recruiter at Thisco, to follow-up on a resume she sent. As luck would have it, Jill herself answers the phone. Jill then asks Lauren a perfectly reasonable question, "Why are you interested in Thisco?" Lauren's prospects with Thisco will be significantly enhanced if she can indicate some positive facts about Thisco and what motivated her to apply for a position.

How could Lauren (or you) be prepared for a situation like this? I suggest making a thumb nail sketch of each firm to which you are applying. Include at least some of the following information:

- Company's main products or services.

- Approximate size in revenue or number of employees.

- A piece of corporate culture (e.g. open door policy; horizontal structure).

- A news item related to the company. (Check Tip #93 for sources of information)

Keep these sketches in a binder near your phone. Just prior to making your follow-up call, quickly review the appropriate sketch. Then you will be prepared in the event you are asked a question like Jill's.

TIP #98: Be Prepared For an Unexpected Telephone Call

We are all familiar with the expression "Don't call us, we'll call you." Sometimes, that is exactly what happens. Let's revisit Lauren and Jill:

Lauren's phone rings. "Hello, is this Lauren Kolbach? This is Jill Artsen and I wonder if this is a good time to talk."

If Lauren is unprepared, she will have no idea who Jill is. In fact, Lauren may assume it is a sales call and hang up.

Lauren (and you) should be prepared for an unexpected call from an employer. There are two reasons for a possible call. First, some employers find an initial or screening interview is more cost-effective if conducted by phone rather than face to face. Second, some employers would like to see how you interview without lots of preparation time.

This is what I suggest:

If you are prepared: Catch your breath, sit down and interview.

If you are unprepared: Be pleasant, but try to defer. Lauren might say, "Jill it's great to hear from you! I am glad you are interested in speaking with me, but this is a bad moment. Can we arrange another time to speak?"

The advantage of this approach is that Lauren will get a chance to compose herself and do some preparation. A drawback is that Lauren loses the opportunity to impress Jill with her state of preparedness without prior notice. In addition, some recruiters may not bother to call you again.

On balance, being prepared and interviewing on the spot is the best approach. However, if you are unprepared or simply cannot speak with the recruiter at that moment, defer.

If you use an answering machine, make sure your voice mail message sounds upbeat and professional. Bizarre messages may seem humorous to you, but they tend to leave negative impressions with recruiters.

TIP #99: Acing a Telephone Interview

To control expenses, some firms will conduct at least the initial screening interview over the phone. The firm's minimum goal is to eliminate the obviously inappropriate candidates. Your minimum goal is to prove yourself to be not obviously inappropriate. Here are some tips for acing the telephone interview.

- Prepare as you would for any other interview. The fact that the main characters are unable to see each other doesn't change the basic rules.

- Form a mental image of a bright, friendly person on the other end of the phone.

- Have your resume handy in case you want to refer to it.

- Have paper handy in case you want to take notes.

- Have some good questions to ask.

- Let your voice show enthusiasm.

- Be prepared for an interview lasting from fifteen minutes to one-half hour.

Silence is not a bad sign. Don't stumble over yourself trying to end a silence at the other end of the phone.

Since your body language, so to speak, will be in your voice, it is a good idea to get a bit pumped before the interview begins. Remember, this interview is a business meeting.

TIP #100: Confidentiality

For people who currently hold a job, looking for a new position is sometimes a bit dicey. You want prospective employers to consider you for an interview without your current employer considering you disloyal. What should you do with your resume if your boss shouldn't know you are looking?

Box numbers: Don't respond to a help wanted situation where the prospective employer is not explicitly identified. The box number could belong to your current employer. Responding to a help wanted advertisement which identifies only a box number is a case of poor judgment, unless your are currently unemployed.

Employment agencies: If you are using an employment agency, retain control of your resume. For example, insist that your approval be given prior to having your resume shared with any prospective employer. Absent that guarantee, either utilize the protections described below or don't use that agency.

Data bases: Inquire about methods to block out your name. Assigning you a number is one method which is sometimes used. In addition you may want to use a descriptor in place of the actual name of your current or past employers. After all, being the applicant who is Vice President for Marketing at CheeseKing Products hardly protects your identity even if your "name" is listed as #2468. Use a descriptor like this: **"Marketing Vice President for a large consumer edible corporation."**

Being cautious makes sense; being paranoid doesn't. Taken to the extreme, you wouldn't apply for a new job at all. On the other hand, an earnest discussion of your career plans with your manager may be possible without jeopardizing your current job. In such cases, concern about confidentiality is much less important.

TIP #101: Discouragement and Complacency

Discouragement

For most people receiving "no interest" letters is far more common than being invited to an interview. It is easy to become discouraged. Here are some ideas for maintaining your morale.

- **Add irons to the fire:** Applying for new jobs should be part of your weekly routine. Knowing that your resume is being reviewed by 5 or 10 additional employers every week helps maintain morale and lessens your anxiety about any one specific employment situation.

- **Pursue information interviews:** They tend to be easier to arrange and keep you actively involved with people in the field. Information interviews can also generate job leads. (See Tip #22)

- **Be realistic:** A good resume will open interview doors, but maybe not on your first or second try. You are likely to hear "no" more often than "yes." But you will get to "yes," and you only need one job at a time.

Complacency

When Barry asked what Larry was doing with his job search, Larry said, "I have two interviews scheduled for the end of the month." Barry was glad for Larry, but asked, "What are you doing between now and then?" Larry was preparing for his forthcoming interviews (a vital effort in itself) but he had stopped applying for other jobs.

Having interviews on your schedule is no reason to stop searching for additional opportunities. After all, an interview is not a job offer and you may not accept the job even if it is offered. Besides, knowing that you are creating more options will help you face the interviews you have scheduled with less anxiety.

Let's take the job search process one more step. Your resume has earned an interview for a wonderful job. Your interview goes well, the job is offered and you accept it. Now picture this scene. The curtain goes up on your first day of work. Do not expect to hear applause from your employer. On the contrary, your audience will be expecting a great performance. Winning the job is a chance to do the job. Applause will come when you have done the job well.

12

Sample Resumes

In the previous chapters we looked at 101 quick tips for writing a dynamite resume. The chapter constitutes a bonus Tip, #101, with seventeen resumes designed for individuals in various job search situations. These resumes are intended to provide ideas for your own resume. They should not be viewed as models to be copied.

Max in Brief

Max has been the senior purchasing manager for a medium sized manufacturer, Gadgetco, for seven years. He has a staff of six. His value to the firms rests heavily on his ability to identify least cost suppliers of essential materials. Max has sharpened his skills in analyzing costs, which includes factors such as quality control and reliable delivery. In addition, Max has been a good negotiator, securing the best available terms from suppliers. Within Gadgetco, Max has maintained good relations with line managers, for whom quality and reliability are paramount, and with the Treasurer, for whom bottom line profit/loss is life's passion.

Max is considering a change and is looking seriously at a consulting firm, GSF Associates, which specializes in corporate engineering. GSF Associates is a privately held concern. It doesn't issue an annual report. However, it actively seeks new clients. To that end, it publishes marketing materials touting its services. In addition, GSF's partners are available to the business press for the purpose of offering sage observations which become free publicity when cited in print. Based on these sources, Max constructed this picture of GSF, utilizing *their own words* as much as possible:

What GSF Associates Seeks From Its Consultants

GSF Associates serves clients striving to remain competitive and increase profitability by "re-engineering" the company. Re-engineering means finding ways of reorganizing the company's processes to produce their marketable product at a lower cost but with the same or greater level of quality. GSF goes beyond finding a better way. It also works with clients to make sure that the current employees don't obstruct or sabotage change.

GSF's clients are divided between service and manufacturing firms, but they do not reveal the percentage breakdown.

Based on his research, Max matched the needs of GSF with his positive characteristics. Max constructed a chart like this one:

GFS needs	My Positive Characteristics
■ Lower cost modes of producing same quality but less expensive products and services ■ Constructive, trusting relationship with client employees	■ Achieve lower cost through **research and negotiations**: (Supplies and materials at same quality but lower cost) ■ Excellent interpersonal skills

From his chart, Max saw that his skills in **researching** sources and **negotiating** with suppliers met GFS's first need (i.e., producing at a lower cost). His **interpersonal skills** in building consensus addressed GFS's philosophy of bringing the client's current employees on board. These positive attributes should be prominently presented by being in Max's Summary.

The Summary below includes the characteristics Max's chart identified while adding nothing extraneous. Even the position Max is seeking fits GFS nicely.

Summary: Reduced costs while maintaining quality. Negotiated with external suppliers and developed consensus with internal managers. Research on alternatives led to greater competitiveness. Seeks to contribute skills gained as a line manager in a consulting environment.

Utilizing his Summary as a roadmap for writing and knowing the importance of connecting his Summary and Experience, Max wrote his Experience this way:

PROFESSIONAL EXPERIENCE

GADGETCO - **Senior Purchasing Manager** (1996 - Present)
Austin, Texas

Reduced costs by $1.2 million while maintaining quality of supplies:

- Research new supply options including "out-sources"

- Negotiated with suppliers for lowest feasible prices while attaining commitment to our specifications.

- Built consensus among production managers before switching suppliers

Voted "Employee of the Year" for making firm more competitive without dismissing employees. (1997) Promoted to current position after only one year as assistant. (1990 - present)

- **Assistant Purchasing Manager** (1995)
- **Inventory Clerk** (1992-95)

Max's experience has a number of strengths

- Demonstrates professional advancement.

- Highlights his ability to save his employer money. This is a virtue in any business but of special significance to consultants offering a re-engineering service.

- Places Max's positive characteristics at the front of each statement (e.g., reduced costs, researched, negotiated, built consensus)

- Shows sensitivity to employee anxiety by **explanation of why** Max was voted Employee of the Year.

- Mentions "outsourcing," a frequent part of re-engineering.

- Max also bolded his current and previous titles, to make his career progress easier to see in a quick reading.

However, Max's experience also contains two weaknesses.

- Max has forgotten to show results in any of his bullet statements.

- Max has forgotten to show context, e.g., the relative significance of Max's $1.2 million reduction in purchasing. Max corrects these weaknesses as shown on page 133.

EDUCATION

UNIVERSITY OF MASSACHUSETTS (Amherst)
Bachelor of Arts   June 1992
Major: History   Minor: philosophy

In the few lines of his Education, Max will tell the recruiter:

- Max studied at a good college

- Max went to work for Gadgetco after graduation (e.g., Max graduated in June, 1990 and started to work in 1990). That explains why Gadgetco is the only cited work experience.

- The study of history and philosophy implies an interest in probing situations, asking pertinent questions and challenging shallow answers. These are excellent attributes in a consultant. Thus Max's college major and minor might be an asset in this case. However, if Max is seeking a different kind of job he might skip mentioning his college major and minor, particularly if the prospective employer tends to favor a technical education.

Those three points add value to Max's resume and don't pose any discernible risk.

After Education, Max added two Other Selling Points (OSPs), namely his computer skills and community involvement.

On the next page, you can see one resume Max developed. It clearly shows the progression of his titles, but doesn't correct the weaknesses we noted above. Page 133 presents a resume Max wrote which emphasizes his experience at one firm, Gadgetco, and shows his results more thoroughly.

MAX JORDAN
7373 Hamlet Drive
Austin, TX 78759
H (512) 489-1776
W (512) 749-1881

Summary: Reduced costs while maintaining quality. Negotiated with external suppliers and developed consensus with internal managers. Research on alternative sources resulted in more secure, less expensive supply sources.

PURCHASING EXPERIENCE

Senior Purchasing Manager
Gadgetco, Austin, Texas (1996-present)
Gadgetco is a $400 million manufacturer of precision handtools.

Reduced costs by $1.2 million while maintaining quality of supplies:

- Researched alternatives to identify new options including outsourcing.
- Negotiated with suppliers for lowest feasible prices while attaining commitment to our specifications.
- Built consensus among production managers before switching suppliers.
- Voted "Employee of the Year" for making firm more competitive without dismissing employees.
- Promoted to current position after only one year as assistant.

Assistant Purchasing Manager
Gadgets, Austin, Texas (1995)

Inventory Clerk
Gadgets, Austin, Texas (1992-95)

EDUCATION

UNIVERSITY OF TEXAS (EL PASO)
Bachelor of Arts　　　　　May, 1990
Major: History　　　　Minor: Philosophy

Computer Skills: Datacrunch, Veritas, C++; Extensive use of Internet

Community Involvements: Active in Austin Chamber of Commerce and Big Brothers

Max Jordan
737 Hamlet Drive
Austin, TX 78759
H 489-1776
W 749-1881

Summary: Reduced costs while maintaining quality. Negotiated with external suppliers and developed consensus with internal managers. Research on alternatives lead to greater competitiveness. Seeks to contribute skills gained as line manager in a consulting environment.

PROFESSIONAL EXPERIENCE: (1990 - present)

GADGETCO - **Senior Purchasing Manager**
Austin, Texas (1996 - present)

Reduced costs by $1.2 million (8% of operating budget) while maintaining quality of supplies:

- Researched alternatives to identify new options including "out-sources"; Restructured purchasing arrangements for 40% of supplies

- Negotiated with suppliers for lowest feasible prices while attaining commitment to our specifications. Obtained average of 10% reduction in costs with continuing suppliers

- Built consensus among production managers before switching suppliers.

Voted "Employee of the Year" for making firm more competitive without dismissing employees. (1997) Promoted to current position after only one year as assistant.

- **Assistant Purchasing Manager** (1995)
- **Inventory Clerk** (1992-95)

EDUCATION
UNIVERSITY OF MASSACHUSETTS

Bachelor or Arts   May, 1990
Major: History   Minor: Philosophy

Computer Skills: Datacrunch; Veritas; C++

Community Involvements: Active in civic and charitable affairs

Shelly Engineers a Resume

Shelly LeMaster is in a fortunate position. She has education and experience in a hot profession, namely electrical engineering. To maximize the impact of her resume (pages 135-136), Shelly made sure to demonstrate her business sensitivities and teamwork skills in addition to her technical expertise.

Shelly has used italics when making a statement about the general nature of her positions or results she achieved. In her case, italics make her resume more pleasant to read and easier to understand. Shelly realizes that if her resume is scanned by an Optical Character Reader (OCR) her italicized statements may not be read properly. For Shelly the advantage gained when her resume is read by a person (which is still the most common case) outweighs the risk of a scanning problem with an OCR.

Lauren Re-enters the Job Market

As Lauren considered possible career paths to pursue when she re-entered the job market, physician practice group management was high on her list. She had seen a news report about the profession and followed up by researching the field through the appropriate professional association Web sites on the Internet (Tips #88 and #89). Then she arranged an information interview with a practitioner in the field (Tip #22). The practitioner and Lauren reviewed some of the job descriptions Lauren had downloaded from Web sites or read in the help wanted section of the local newspaper. Together they identified several which met the dual criteria Lauren had wisely set. First, the job description appealed to Lauren. Second, Lauren felt reasonably confident that she could do the job. At the top of page 137 is one of the job descriptions Lauren and the practitioner identified.

SHELLY LEMASTER
41 Fox Glove Dr.
Rosewell, Georgia 30076
(770) 576-1834
slmaster@aol.com

Objective: Continue building career in software engineering

Professional Qualifications: Eight years of electrical engineering experience including design and quality assurance. Excellent teamwork, technical and analytical skills.

ENGINEERING EXPERIENCE
Nanochip, Inc.   Roswell,
GA
Project Engineer   1996-
Present
  Member of four department team evaluating manufacturing software for the metal industry.

- Conduct tests utilizing electronic testers and dry runs
- Analyze volumes of test data
- Identify problem spots and recommend solutions

Resulted in software which reaches end-users 98.7% glitch free on or before promised delivery date

Consulting Engineer   1995-96

- Researched product development and testing cycle
- Identified redundant and inefficient steps
- Recommended six step program of improvement

Resulted in a software development process which minimized frustration among developers, incorporated more input from end-users early on, and saved an average of $150,000 per program.

Wright Precision Gizmos   Durham, NC

Service Engineer   1993-95

Designed software systems and supervised implementation on the shop floor for this $600 million industrial gizmos producer

- Developed software which reduced manufacturing defects by 15%
- Identified equipment and software modifications needed to produce new orders to specification
- Cooperated with machine workers to eliminate software snags

Resulted in 50% reduction in capital costs per unit sold

Electronics Technician   1992-93

- Installed new software systems
- Take-offs from blueprint for assembly-line machines

EDUCATION

Bachelor of Science in Electrical Engineering   1992
Edison University, Wayne, NJ

Assistant Executive Director

Assists the top administrator in planning, directing and coordinating non-patient care activities. May have limited responsibilities in marketing and recruiting. Our medical practice has three Assistant Executive Directors who frequently work as a team. Reports to Executive Director, our top non-medical position.

Lauren wrote a resume for Assistant Executive Director with a physicians' practice group, trying to show those positive characteristics the job description identified; i.e., planning, directing, coordinating, marketing, recruiting and team work. Lauren did not have all these characteristics but she identified some close substitutes: "Fund raising" for marketing; "persuaded" for recruiting and "involving 20 volunteers" for "teamwork." In addition, she included some useful generic positive characteristics which weren't requested in the job description, namely complying with government regulations, flexibility and leadership.

Lauren's physicians' practice group resume is on the next page. This style of resume may not scan very well. However physicians' practice groups tend to be relatively small and therefore probably don't use scanners, so Linda was not concerned. A person applying to a very large firm or a firm hiring computer specialists or engineers would be better advised not to use this format.

Lauren also noted on her Summary that she had taken time out to finish raising her family. She decided to mention family responsibilities to explain work gaps on her resume. The fact that she had *finished* raising her family should minimize any adverse prejudices about family responsibilities.

Lauren Smithfield
93 Devonshire Drive
Happy Valley, MI 48109
(413) 584-9854

Summary: Planning, organization and communication skills. Proven leader; goal oriented but flexible. Returning to workforce after time-out to finish raising my family. Seeks administrative position in a physicians' practice group.

ADMINISTRATIVE EXPERIENCE
Very Good Product, Inc.- Haventown, PA
Excellent Eateries - Media, PA
Demonstrated flexibility by moving among six different functional areas to substitute for vacationing employees. Responded to customer inquiries, built files on EXCEL and developed basic financial reports using Lotus. Learned about specific business concerns in office supply and restaurant industries. Found positions through Excel Temporary Help Agency. (1997).

MANAGEMENT EXPERIENCE
Vice President
Singing for At-Risk Children (SARC) - Detroit, MI
Planned annual conference for individual and corporate sponsors. Organized concert tours for at risk children served by Foundation. Spoke to civic gatherings and media to publicize SARC. Complied with government regulations and detailed by-laws while building 600 client organization. Promoted four times in three years (1985-1988).

LEADERSHIP EXPERIENCE
Vice President: Happy Valley PTO - Michigan
Directed fund raising campaign involving 20 volunteers which yielded $250,000 in labor, materials and cash for a new recreational facility. Persuaded local merchants to donate material in exchange for good will. Researched fund raising techniques using the Internet. Created Access file of contributors (1996-98).
President: Royal Bear Civic Association: Elected because of excellent management and leadership skills. (1992-94)

EDUCATION
Escola College, Meriden, CT
Bachelor of Arts, 1985
Major: Communications; Graduated *cum laude*
Computer Skills: Access, Excel, Lotus

Comments On Lauren Smithfield's Resume

Strengths

- A Clear Career Goal—stated in her Summary
- Category Format—Good idea since Lauren has been out of the work force. (Tip #27)
- Positive Characteristics—Stated in Summary: supporting examples given in Experience. (Tip #21)
- Easy to Read—Spacing and bolding show logical categories and make resume pleasant to the eye. (Tip #26)

Weakness

- Some recruiters may feel that any mention of "family" may be more appropriate in a cover letter than on a resume, if it is to be mentioned at all.

Marilyn's Story

Marilyn became a stockbroker after several years as a K-12 school teacher. Marilyn wants a resume which emphasizes her current profession and de-emphasizes her previous one. This is almost a mirror image of Lauren's strategy (see page 134) which *relied on her past history* to build credibility.

Marilyn's resume is on the next page. Notice that she referred to her previous career in one line at the end of her resume. When a person's previous career ended a while ago but might raise some skeptical eyebrows in their current field, this is a good strategy.

Marilyn gives her e-mail address at work in her heading. This is acceptable **if** private use of company e-mail will not result in disciplinary action **and** Marilyn is the only person who can access her e-mail.

Marilyn Nasdow
9763 Kornfield Road
Cedar Rapids, IA
(319) 867-1438
mnas@ejthom.com

BUSINESS EXPERIENCE

E.J. Thomson   Cedar Rapids, IA
Financial Advisor   1993-Present
Successful fee and commission-based sales for this full service brokerage.

- Advise clients on best investment strategies to meet retirement needs and college education costs.

- Sell common stocks and mutual funds based on client needs.

- Manage six client portfolios on an annual fee basis.

- Gross commissions #1 or #2 in branch of thirty advisors for three consecutive years

Summerville Pools   Sioux City, IA
Sales Representative   1991-1993

- Sold full range of pools and maintenance services.

- Prospected clients including private homes, apartment complexes and small municipalities.

- Built client base through low cost promotional events which gained media coverage.

Prior to 1991—High School Teacher—Cedar Rapids, Iowa.

EDUCATION

University of Sioux City   Iowa
Bachelor of Arts

Computer Skills: Quarryplus; Marketwatch, Access.

Rhonda Redux

During the course of this book we had the opportunity to learn a good deal about Rhonda, an experienced marketing professional looking for her next career opportunity in her current field. Due to her wealth of directly related professional experience and her relatively high level position, Rhonda has decided that a two page resume, presented on pages 142-143, makes most sense for her.

Comments On Rhonda Franklin's Resume

Strengths

- Clear Focus
- Logical Progression
- Achievement Oriented

Weakness

- Doubt: Scope of supervisory experience

Possible Modification

Rhonda has laudatory statements about her skills and accomplishments at the beginning of her resume. **This is an unconventional approach to resume writing.** But Rhonda is a bit of a risk taker who wishes to indicate her willingness to take a carefully considered chance. "Besides," Rhonda said, "I wouldn't want to work for anyone who would not interview me based on this resume format." If Rhonda had wished to be more cautious, she could put these laudatory remarks at the end of her resume or under references. In that case she could even put the appropriate phone numbers with the advance permission of the individuals involved.

Rhonda Franklin
293 Wildflower Drive
Minneapolis, MN 55402
(612) 973-1256 (H)
(612) 584-4121
email: rfranklin@aol.com

"Her creativity is matched by her skill in precise implementation. Rhonda has enabled us to cut the lead time in bringing products to market by six months" (1997 Annual Performance Review).

"Rhonda has been a critical factor in returning our division to profitability." (William Tiller, Vice President of Widget Home Appliance division.)

MARKETING EXPERIENCE (1988-present)

Consumer Delight Corporation   Austin, TX
Manager of Planning   (1993-Present)

Four years of increasing responsibilities experience with this $.6 billion consumer products company.

Achievements:

- Inaugurated Tough Toe Nail line. Added $20 million annually to the bottom line which added $20 million annually to company's profit.
- Reduced product design and advertising costs by $2 million (15%) using PIMS.
- Integrated teams of marketing, finance and logistic staff which accelerated introduction of products to market.
- Developed contingency plan to deal with possibility of stagnant economic growth.

Responsibilities:

- Determine new product lines consistent with company's strategic goals
- Forecast future potential of current products
- Supervise staff of four analysts and two planners who track production costs and price points

Widget Corp. - Home Appliance Division   Dayton, OH
Director of Forecasting   (1991-1993)

First marketing forecaster for this $.5 billion consumer durable product firm.

Achievements:

- Forecasted demand by product and demographic segment reduced need for production overtime by $200,000 (10%).

Rhonda Franklin, Page 2

- Identified potential areas for product differentiation; Resulted in repositioned mid-range products.
- Reduced unsold inventory by accurate analysis of cycles for main products.

Responsibilities:

- Analyzed macroeconomic demographic and consumer data
- Monitored actual sales against previous forecasts
- Reported monthly to senior management with recommendations for changes in market strategies.

Beautiful Basics, Inc.   Windsor, CT
Senior Marketing Analyst   (1988-1993)

Promoted rapidly due to excellent analytical and interpersonal skills which benefited this privately-held pillow company.

Achievements:

- Identified data for predicting pillow purchases from sleep patterns.
- Recommended optimal channels of distribution, reducing logistic costs.
- Began as Marketing Assistant; promoted more quickly to current position than any predecessor in company.

Responsibilities:

- Researched primary and secondary sources to identify best reliable data available at minimum costs.
- Managed "Secret Shopper" program.
- Collect data and anecdotal evidence from sales force.

EDUCATION

Bachelor of Business Administration, May 1988
University of Connecticut (Storrs)
Major: Marketing   Minor: Statistics

Computer Skills - Internet for consumer research; Excel, Markatel, Datacrunch.

Personal - Active in local chapters of American Marketing Association and National Sleep Tight organization

Life After College

Larry, our forthcoming college graduate, is considering two possible career paths. One is in market research. For this situation, Larry stresses his "hardworking, realistic, self starter" character, in part to address the potential objection that he lacks the commercial, results driven nature of that field. Larry also stresses his skills in research, questionnaire design and surveying, since these skills would be fundamental in market research. He devotes considerable space to two of his group projects in college, since they demonstrate some of the skills a market research firm would want.

At the same time, Larry is considering a career in the non-profit sector. From a friend, Larry heard of an opportunity with a group called *Save the Panda* and has designed a different resume for that purpose. This organization focuses on public awareness rather than voting and *Save the Panda* is interested in publicity, an area in which Larry has no direct experience. To address this possible objection as best he can, Larry rewrote and repositioned one of his college group projects and introduced new information to his National Chain and Saw experience because of its connection to the needs of *Save the Panda*.

Larry's market research resume is on the next page, followed by his *Save the Panda* resume.

Larry Kandola

College Address
76 Heritage Drive
South Hadley, MA 01007
(413) 584-1773
ekandola@mtherald.edu

Permanent Address
93 Faunce Street
Philadelphia, PA 19152
(215) 742-9381

Summary: Hardworking, realistic, self-starter. Solid analytical and communication skills. Combines solid education with practical work experience. Seeks position in Market Research.

EDUCATION:
Mt. Herald College, South Hadley, MA
Bachelor of Arts   May, 1999
Major: Political Theory   Overall GPA 3.2

Group Projects:

Researched student voter participation as part of four person team. Wrote detailed proposal for increasing overall political participation. Resulted in establishment of a polling district on campus and formation of student advocacy group on behalf of College (Spring, 1997).
Designed questionnaire to identify major trends in student political thinking. Persuaded representative sample to devote time to giving extended responses. Conclusions reported in the daily campus newspaper (Fall, 1996).

Worked 25 hours per week during academic periods. Self-financed 90% of college living expenses.

Computer Skills: Dbase, Lotus, Excel, Powerpoint, SPSS
Activities: Intramural softball; student senator.

Honors:
   Alpha Beta Gamma Society—In recognition of outstanding contributions to campus historical preservation.
   Einstein Memorial—Awarded to student who best exemplifies the Theory of Relativity in daily life.

EXPERIENCE
National Saw and Chain - Agawam, MA
Surveyed employees to identify perceptions of fringe benefits package. Designed questionnaire to maximize response rate while capturing critical information. Analyzed data to identify patterns and potential problems. Reported to Vice President of Human Resources on conclusions and recommendations. Commended for bringing enthusiasm and fresh ideas. (Internship - Fall 1997)

Sam's Nutritious Delights, Belchertown, MA.
Worked evenings and weekends, averaging 25 hours per week during academic semesters. Doubled as waiter and dishwasher as circumstances warranted. Praised by manager for hard work and reliability. Noted by customers for fast, friendly, effective service (Fall, Spring 1996-98)

Other Positions: Brick layer (Summer, 1997); Recreation Counselor (Summer 1996)

Activities: Junior Chamber of Commerce—speakers bureau.

Larry Kandola

College Address
76 Heritage Drive
South Hadley, MA
(413) 584-1773

Permanent Address
93 Faunce Street
Philadelphia, PA 19152
(215) 742-9381

Summary: Hardworking, realistic, self-starter. Solid analytic and communication skills. Combines social science education with commitment to public service. Seeks position with a public service advocacy group.

EDUCATION:
Mt. Herald College, South Hadley, MA
Bachelor of Arts   May, 1999
Major: Political Theory   Overall GPA 3.2

> **Worked 25 hours per week during academic periods. Self-financed 90% of college living expenses.**

Group Projects:

- Formed student advocacy group as one result of a research project on voter participation.
- Wrote detailed proposal for increasing overall political participation. (Spring, 1997)
- Identified major trends in student political thinking. Persuaded representative sample to participate in study. Convinced daily campus newspaper to report results; given two columns of coverage.

Computer Skills: Dbase, Lotus, Excel, Powerpoint, SPSS
Activities: Intramural softball; student senator.

Honors:
   Alpha Beta Gamma Society—In recognition of outstanding contributions to campus historical preservation.
   Einstein Memorial—Awarded to student who best exemplifies the Theory of Relativity in daily life.

WORK EXPERIENCE:
National Saw and Chain - Agawam, MA
- Surveyed employees to identify perceptions of fringe benefits package.
- Uncovered a variety of concerns through designing and administering questionnaire.
- Analyzed data to identify patterns and potential problems. Reported to Vice President of Human Resources on conclusions and recommendations. Commended for bringing enthusiasm and fresh ideas. (Internship- Fall 1997).

Sam's Nutritious Delights, Belchertown, MA
- Worked evenings and weekends, averaging 25 hours per week during academic semesters. Doubled as waiter and dishwasher as circumstances warranted. Praised by manager for hard work and reliability. Noted by customers for fast, friendly, effective service (Fall, Spring 1996-98)

Other Positions: Brick layer (Summer, 1997); Recreation Counselor (Summer, 1996).

Activities: Junior Chamber of Commerce–speakers bureau.

About Beth

Beth is a highly competent, technically oriented individual. She meets or exceeds the expectations. That is one reason Beth placed Experience before Education on her resume. There is a second reason: Beth never really liked school very much and so she did not go to college. Her next employer may well be expecting a person with a technical college degree, perhaps in engineering. Beth has the talent but not the diploma. Therefore it makes sense for Beth to make Education less prominent. Her resume appears on page 148.

Beth Golden
96 Holten Road
Bismarck, North Dakota
(701) 247-9853

Career Goal: To continue career in the Technical Service Industry.

TECHNICAL SERVICE EXPERIENCE
Technical Service Manager   (1996-Present)
Laser Guided Production, Bismarck, ND
Provide customers throughout western US with training and logistic support.
- Train installation and maintenance crews
- Respond to technical inquires from clients and sales staff
- Supervise installations for large clients

Service Technician
Computer Wizards, Inc.   (1993-1996)
Fargo, ND
Repaired work station computers and LAN's for this $750 million high-tech manufacturer
- Praised by clients for excellent problem solving skills and on-time service.
- Praised by management for expertise and cooperation with other departments, especially marketing.

Production
Printing Palace, Inc.
Chevy Chase, MD
Designed high-end printers and mass mailers. Awarded two patents

MILITARY EXPERIENCE
United States Navy (1988-1992)
Petty Officer Second Class
Fundamentals of Submarine Search; Track and Attack Methods
Electronic Maintenance Specialist
Special Training: Radar Theory; Acoustic Anti-Submarine Warfare;
Deployed in Keflank, Iceland and Sigonella, Sicily

Honorable Discharge; Navy Achievement Medal

EDUCATION
Certified for Electronic and Mechanical Maintenance 2000 Hours: Specialized Equipment Training High School Diploma

Computer skills: JAVA, Scimpy, Html, C++

Some Background On Harry

Harry is a consultant specializing in marketing strategies for mid-sized firms. He has established a client base which is sufficient to make his enterprise profitable. However, the long work week and the constant need to find new clients are beginning to wear Harry down. Harry is considering the possibility of working full time as a marketing manager for a mid to large size company. As Harry wrote his resume, he kept in mind the need to overcome a possible objection (see Tip #38): "If you are doing so well on your own, why do you want to give up your own business; if you are *not* doing well, why should we consider you?" His two page resume appears on pages 149-150.

Harry decided on a two page resume so that his accomplishments would precede his current mode of employment. Page 1 would exhibit his accomplishments. There Harry wants to demonstrate a close connection with his desired position by emphasizing "Marketing" rather than the fact that his most recent experience is in consulting rather than line management. Page 2 would discuss his consulting practice.

Harry Goodman

1739 North Aberdeen Street
Philadelphia, PA 19149-1357
Phone (215) 338-2550
e-mail: HGG60541@aol.com

SUMMARY

Marketing professional with proven track record in several industries. Increased customer bases, reduced operating expenses, designed both conventional and avant-garde marketing plans.

MARKETING ACCOMPLISHMENTS

- Increased customer base 15% by repositioning product line. (Twisted Pretzel Company).

- Designed marketing plan which increased repeat business by 25%–without price incentives. (Advanced Ironsmith Products).

- Reduced customer capture cost by refining market research database. (Basic Offices, Inc.)

- Developed direct marketing campaign which yielded 9% response rate in a previously untapped market. (Zenda's Print & Copy, LLP).

- Designed website which increased industrial customer contacts by 40%. (Advanced Ironsmith Products).

- Trained sales and service staff to be pro-active and efficient. (PPQ Assembly and Shipping).

- Managed new product release. (Twisted Pretzel Company).

Harry Goodman, page 2

MARKETING EXPERIENCE

Marvels of Marketing, Inc.   Media, PA
President   (1992 - Present)

Consulting service for clients in retail outlets light industry, office supplies.

Selected List of Clientele:

- Advanced Ironsmith Products
- Basic Office, Inc.
- Happy Days Shopping Malls, Inc.
- PDQ Assembly and Shipping
- Zenda's Print & Copy, LLP

TWISTED PRETZEL COMPANY   New Brunswick, NJ
Director of Marketing   (1990-1992)

Repositioned major product line, resulting in 15% increase of customer base. Managed new product release from start to finish which added $18 million (10%) to annual profit. Consolidated sales territories and introduced computer system which resulted in $7 million annual savings in administrative expenses. Served on several senior staff level committees.

Sales Manager   (1987-1990)

Large Client Sales   (1985-1987)

EDUCATION

Middle Tennessee State University (Murfreesboro)
Bachelor of Business Administration May, 1985

Major: Marketing   Minor: Statistics

Computer Skills: Marketmax, Powerpoint, SPSS, HTML

References: Available Upon Request.

David's Category Resume

David is another member of our Job Search Club whose career plans were discussed earlier in this book. On the following page is David's category resume designed to call attention to his experience in both finance and technology.

David Greene
84 Dorothy Way
Fairfax, VA 22037
(H) (703) 665-1743
(W) (703) 787-1991

SUMMARY: Experienced business professional. Praised by manager as "diligent, insightful, thorough, highly respected." Excellent analytical and writing skills. Interested in contributing financial skills in a high-tech environment.

PROFESSIONAL EXPERIENCE:

Finance
Credit Commercial Bank   Fairfax, VA
Credit/Loan Analyst
- Analyze credit worthiness of commercial loan applicants including start-up computer software companies and established enterprises. Range of loans is $5 - $25 million.
- Determine level of risk given a variety of scenarios
- Advise loan committee of recommendations, including interest rates and applicable conditions
- Document loan decisions for internal/external auditors and regulatory agencies (1995-present)

Technology
Gizmo Computer Storage Device   Bethesda, MD
Programmer Trainee
- Trained in programming languages including C+T
- Wrote code for part of data storage microchip (1994-95)

Professional Certifications:
Certified Financial Analyst (1997)
Certified Management Accountant (1995)

Professional Awards
Ofie Trophy: For exceptional risk management (1997)
Hack Plaque: For outstanding use of computer innovations (1995)

Computer Skills: C++, Pascal, Schewe, Excel

EDUCATION

Bachelor of Science   May, 1995
Colorado College (Denver)
Major: Computer Information Systems   Minor: Economics

Gabrielle Goes For the Gold

As we have discussed throughout this book. Gabrielle is looking for a career move within her current profession. She had decided not to mention explicitly her deep interest in Talking Horse Syndrome in her general resume. However, if Gabrielle does apply to a research institute or commercial firm concerned with this rare disease, she could indicate "Has a special interest in Talking Horse Syndrome" at the end of her professional objective.

Gabrielle D'Agostino
345 Settlement Road
Winston-Salem, NC 27116
(910) 768-9297 e-mail: GDA15047@aol.com

PROFESSIONAL QUALIFICATIONS
Research and analytical skills demonstrated in both commercial and academic setup. Competent with even the most sophisticated equipment and techniques

PROFESSIONAL OBJECTIVE
Seek research position in laboratory dedicated to preventing or curing human diseases

MICROBIOLOGY EXPERIENCE
Cellmate, Inc.   Winston-Salem, NC
Project Researcher   1994-present
Praised by project manager for timely, useful reports and adherence to budget constraints

- Researching impact of trial antibiotics on a variety of microorganisms for this $100 million pharmaceutical company (1997-present)
- Analyzed laboratory data to identify possible correlations between smog levels and hyperactive vocal cord cells (1996-97)
- Designed studies to test cell defenses against effects of dioxin (1995-1996)
- Measured changes in cell growth under a variety of hormone inputs (1994-95)

Gained expertise in use of both basic and sophisticated equipment, including Cellatrope and Nanoscope

EDUCATION

Master of Science: Microbiology   **May, 1994**
University of Redwoods, Glenmark, CA

Master Research Project:

The Influence of Enzymes on Neural Inhibitors–Analyzed existing data on neural inhibitors. Designed experiments to identify possible enzymes for inhibiting dysfunctional neural transmissions.

Bachelor of Science: Microbiology   **May, 1990**
University of Texas - El Paso
   Developed excellent technical and laboratory research skills
Computer skills: Microstat, Datacrunch, Selcell

The Story of Roslyn Riveter

Some people work full-time for a number of years prior to completing college or another educational goal. Roslyn is a case in point. As a younger person, Roslyn didn't like academic study very much so she entered the work force at 18 years of age. As years went by, Roslyn decided that she wanted to change to a white collar position, but her lack of a college degree stood in her way.

Roslyn decided to study in a community college at night. She did well, enjoying academic work far more than she had as a younger person. In fact, Roslyn pursued a bachelor's degree after she received her associates degree from the community college.

Roslyn was proud of her work experience. She had demonstrated reliability and initiative. The possibility of utilizing her transportation experience as a drawing card appealed to Roslyn, so she wrote one of her resumes for this field. However, Roslyn didn't want to dwell on the details of her work life, especially since she hoped to enter a different kind of profession. Therefore, Roslyn decided to have a Summary which indicated some important positive characteristics, a statement about her work experience before college and her professional goals now that she had graduated. Since her recent degree was such an important achievement, Roslyn placed Education prior to Experience.

The next page shows the resume Roslyn wrote for a transportation job in *private industry*.

Roslyn Riveter
97 Hardrock Drive
Allentown, PA 18036
(601)545-9397

Qualifications: Highly motivated self starter. Excellent planning and organizing skills. Worked for a number of years prior to pursuing a college education.

Objective: Seeks to continue career in transportation logistics.

EDUCATION

Bachelor of Arts	May, 1998
Copton College, Bethlehem, PA	
Major: Statistics	Minor: Transportation

Associates of Arts	May, 1994
King of Prussia Community College (Pennsylvania)	

EXPERIENCE
Transportation

Dispatcher: Heavy Load Trucking (1993-Present)
Determined departure times, routes and appropriate cargoes for 16 truck fleet. Tracked shipment progress. Resolved conflicts between drivers and management.

Driver: Taggett Cargo and Freight (1988-93)
Drove 16 wheel cargo trucks, both long and short haul. Perfect safety record.

Manufacturing

Worked night shift as:
Assembler   Computer Components Inc. (1986-88)
Packager   Mail Order Madness, (1984-86)

Praised by all three managers for excellent work ethic, team work and problem solving ideas.

Computer Skills:
Statismante, Excel, Access, Turbotrans

Professional Associations:
American Trucking Association
American Load Carriers Association

Let's assume that Roslyn is pursuing a position with *the US government*, a career path different from others discussed in this book.

Many federal agencies no longer require the SF-171, a fact which brings tears to the eyes of hardly anyone. Still, these agencies do require a resume which includes more information than would be required (or even desired) outside of government service. Roslyn's resume for federal agencies included the following additional information:

- Title and Announcement number for the position she is seeking

- Citizenship status

- Veteran's preference points

- Salary History

- Name and phone number of applicable supervisor

- References

- Certification of Truth

In addition, Roslyn does not worry about keeping her resume to one page when it is being sent to a US government agency.

Roslyn's government service resume appears on the following pages:

Roslyn Riveter
97 Hardrock Drive
Allentown, PA 18036
(601) 545-9397

Announcement
US DOT 98:07
Logistics Specialist

Qualifications: Highly motivated self starter. Excellent planning and organizing skills. Worked for a number of years prior to pursuing a college education. US citizen with 5 point Veteran Preference (DD-214 attached).
Born: October 15, 1970

Objective: Seeks to build a career in transportation logistics with the US government.

EDUCATION

Bachelor of Arts   May 1998
Copton College, Bethlehem, PA
Major: Statistics   Minor: Transportation

Associates of Arts   May 1994
King of Prussia Community College (Pennsylvania)

EXPERIENCE
Transportation

October 1993-present.   **Dispatcher:** Heavy Load Trucking, Bethlehem, PA
$31,000; Mr. Lon Freight   Determined departure times, routes and appropri-
(610) 934-2200   ate cargoes for 16 truck fleet. Tracked shipment
                                              progress. 40-60 hours/week
                                              Resolved conflicts between drivers and manage
                                              ment.

July 1990-Sept. 1993   **Driver:** Taggett Cargo and Freight, Lake Como, PA
$29,000; Mr.Sam Turner   Drove 16 wheel cargo trucks, both long and short
(610) 272-1971   haul. Perfect safety record.
40-70 hours/week

Manufacturing

March 1989-July 1990   Worked night shift as:
$6.50/hour Don Hunter   **Assembler** Computer Components Inc., Altoona,
(814) 734-9197   PA
45 hours/week

June 1988-March 1989   **Packager** Mail Order Madness, Pittsburgh, PA
$5.30/hour Ms. Ellen Iron
(412) 757-1321
Ms. Samantha Stamper
(412) 757-1335
50 hours/week

Praised by all three managers for excellent work ethic, team work and problem solving ideas.

Military

Pennsylvania National Guard 1988-1992
Honorable Discharge
Rank: Sergeant

Computer Skills:

Statismante, Excel, Lotus, Turbotrans

Professional Associations:
American Trucking Association
American Load Carriers Association

References
Captain John L. Dewey   (610) 934-1737
Ms. Roberta Flax   (610) 843-1300
Mr. Lon Freight   (412) 937-1597

A New Resume, By George

George enjoys his job as an Executive Secretary for a large cereal processor. He focused on his administrative and executive support skills in his resume since they are his potential tickets to an even better job.

George Scott
2675 Grainery Drive
Frozen Pond, MN 55806
(218) 764-1732

Summary: Reliable, efficient, selfstarter seeks to continue career in administration, particularly where word processing, secretarial and organizational skills would be an asset.

PROFESSIONAL EXPERIENCE

Executive Secretary, Multigrain, Inc. Duluth, MN (1996-Present)

- Streamlined operations supporting Vice-President of Finance. Saved $150,000 over three years.

- Wrote correspondence on vice-president's behalf.

- Developed Policy & Procedures manual to facilitate early productivity of new employees.

- Served on Employee Stakeholder and Firm-wide Safety Committees

Office Manager, Tyler Moore Enterprises, Cold Springs, MN (1993-1996)

- Supervised staff of three secretaries and two customer service representatives.

- Enhanced productivity by 15% through better training and reorganization of staff assignments.

- Organized promotional seminars to attract new clients.

Secretary, Holden, Ltd., Grove Point, MN (1991-1993)

- Receptionist and typist duties

Computer Skills: Wordperfect, Scute, Excel, Lotus

EDUCATION

Numerous seminars sponsored by Minnesota Administrative Excellence, Inc. and Great Lakes Associates

Graduate of Grove Point High School

Some Light On Leonard Pekar

On the next page is the resume Leonard wrote for business driven lighting and interior design firms like his current employer. This resume emphasizes his success in adding value to his employer by reducing costs to his clients. Leonard has designed the resume with plenty of white space, allowing the main points to stand out. Through this resume, Leonard would like a recruiter to interview him based on a small number of salient and attractive facts.

While on vacation in Arkansas, Leonard saw a news item about an art museum which was planning to renovate. "I wonder if they need a project director," Leonard thought to himself. "I would love to get closer to my fine arts roots. Besides, I would appreciate the warmer weather."

Leonard called the museum and discovered that a search for a project director was just getting started. Realizing that the scope of the museum's project was an order of magnitude greater than anything he had ever done and that he would be working with a cultural enterprise rather than a business, Leonard wrote a new resume. Specifically, Leonard wanted to show that he could handle the artistic, interpersonal and technical aspects of the job. At the same time, he didn't want to neglect his proven ability to keep an eye on costs as well as quality. With that in mind, Leonard developed a two page resume so he could expand on projects in a way that related to what a museum would need. That resume starts on page 164.

Leonard Pekar
743 Humphrey Blvd.
St. Cloud, MN 55320
(H) (320) 347-1943
(W) (320) 676-1777
lp@Meadco.com.

Qualifications: Practical experience and education resulted in expertise in several areas:

- Interior Design
- Lighting Design
- Project Estimation and Supervision
- Architectural Woodwork

EDUCATION: Bezalel College of Fine Arts, Lincoln, NB
Bachelor of Arts 1989
Major: Design   Minor: Lighting

EXPERIENCE:

Project Supervisor: 1995-Present

Lux Magnus, Inc.,
Bloomington, MN

Managed projects ranging from small business offices to major corporate headquarters

Project Estimator: 1992-95

Ultimate Interiors,
Bloomington, MN

Estimated material and labor costs for a variety of clients, including historical sites and retail businesses. Reduced time and material waste

Lighting Designer:

1989-92 Lutex Home and
Office Products
Minneapolis, MN

Lumens, Corp.
St. Paul, MN

Projects included upscale homes, small businesses and several art galleries

Leonard Pekar, page 2

Accomplishments:

- Increased repeat business by 50% at Lux Magnus
- Reduced time to completion by 15% at Lux Magnus
- Increased profit margin by 10% through detailed and accurate estimates at Ultimate Interiors.
- Reduced re-do costs by 70% at Lumens Corporation.

Computer Skills: CAD, FreeHand, Model Shop, Mac Draft, Write Now, Excel, Lotus

Certifications: Certified Interior Designer
  CEU Credits: Spotting Fakes in Antique Furniture
  Aesthetics & Performance: Finding the Balance
  Lighting Designs for Interview Spaces

Leonard Pekar

743 Humphrey Blvd.
St. Cloud, MN 55320
(H) (320) 347-1943
(W) (320) 676-1777
lp@Meadco.com.

SUMMARY

Combines fine arts education with eight years applied experience in lighting and interior design. Demonstrated expertise in project management which accommodates both aesthetics and utility. Seeks position with museum or similar cultural institution.

EDUCATION

Bezalel College of Fine Arts, Lincoln NE
Bachelor of Arts   1989
Major: Design   Minor: Lighting

Senior Thesis: *Aesthetics, utility, and lights: Can this uneasy trilogy find harmony?*

Vice President: *Art for Art's Sake Society*

Computer Skills
CAD, FreeHand, Model Shop, Mac Draft, Write Now, Excel, Lotus

Certifications: Certified Interior Designer
    CEU Credits: Spotting Fakes in Antique Furniture
    Aesthetics & Performance: Finding the Balance
    Lighting Designs for Interview Spaces

PROJECT MANAGEMENT EXPERIENCE

Project Supervisor
1995-Present
Lux Magnus, Inc.
Bloomington, MN

Managed projects ranging from small business offices to corporate head quarters. Conferred with clients to determine needs and objectives. Designed both overall plans and detailed diagrams. Combined lighting and interior design to create environments which were both beautiful and functional.

Leonard Pekar, page 2

Reduced time to completion by 15% through detailed planning and continuous coordination with client. Increased repeat contracts by 50% due to high level of client satisfaction.

OTHER LIGHTING AND INTERIOR EXPERIENCE

Project Estimator   1992 - 1995
Ultimate Interiors   Bloomington, MN

Estimated material and labor costs for a variety of clients, including historical sites and retail businesses. Reduced time and material waste, benefiting both the firm and its clients financially.

Lighting Designer   1989 - 1992
Lutex Home and Office Products   Minneapolis, MN
Lumens Corp.   St. Paul, MN

Contract employee working part time for each company

Introduced planning and design methods which reduced re-do costs by 70%. Projects included up-scale homes, small businesses and several art galleries.

Personal: Active in Minnesota Arts Council

Willing to relocate, especially to a sunbelt state

13

Writing a Cover Letter That Adds Value to Your Resume

An Extra Tip: Writing a Cover Letter That Adds Value

A good cover letter is an important part of your job search effort. It should **add value** to your resume rather than just repeating it.

Here are five approaches for writing a cover letter which is a value-adding partner to your resume. You could use one or all of them, depending upon your individual situation:

- **Highlight** items which are of particular importance to your prospective employer, but which aren't prominent on your resume.

- **Reframe** items in a way that will connect them immediately to the prospective employer's interests.

- **Add new material** which is relevant to the specific situation of interest to you, but which wasn't on your resume.

- **Motivation**— explain clearly why you want that specific job and that specific company.

- **Address "credibility gap" issues.** You may have a credibility gap on your resume. For example, you studied in Massachusetts, but the employer is in California. In that case explain your connection to California. For example, you have family there or your finance lives there. If the credibility gap is not addressed (hopefully in an upbeat manner) your probability of being invited to an interview is diminished.

The following example illustrates each of these five approaches.

Example of Cover Letter Utilizing All Five Approaches

Ararat Drive
Ancient City, World 10001

October 1, 1998

Ms. Leah Methusala
Vice President - Underwriting
Woodcraft Insurance Company
1849 Golddust Boulevard
San Francisco, CA 94104

Dear Ms. Methusala:

I am interested in becoming an underwriter for Woodcraft Insurance Company. My work experience and education should make me an asset to your firm. For example:

- Expertise in wood products: Built everything from household items to houses.[1]

- Team work: Involved seven people in Ark Management tasks during the Great Flood.[2]

- Analytical skills: Straight "A" student in analytical and quantitative subjects while earning a college degree.[3]

I am particularly attracted to Woodcraft Insurance for several reasons.[4] First, underwriting is a career which combines the analytical and personal skills I enjoy applying. Second, Woodcraft insures products in which I have both a professional and avocational interest. <u>Third</u>, I am planning to settle in the Bay Area after my wedding later this year.[5]

    My resume is enclosed. I will call you next week to see when a meeting can be arranged at your convenience.

Sincerely,

Noah Arkman

Noah Arkman

Encl: Resume

Note to Readers

[1]   Example of Highlighting
[2]   Example of Reframing
[3]   Example of Something New
[4]   Example of Motivation
[5]   Example of addressing a credibility gap (e.g. in this case geography.)

Noah Arkman
Ararat Drive
Ancient City, World 10001
(999) 666-5678
e-mail: narkman@arko.ararat.com

Summary: Proven skills in leadership, communication, and problem solving. Demonstrated ability to assess risk and respond appropriately. Professional experience with The Flood and reconstruction. Seeks to build a career in insurance, with a special interest in flood insurance. Interest developed as a result of leading role played in worst disaster in recorded history.

Work
Experience: *Flood Beater,* WORLD RESCUE, INC.
Led rescue of human and animal life from the Great Flood. Directed reestablishment of human life on earth. Assessed risk of destruction based on heavenly insight and gathering rain clouds. Responded by organizing thousands of creatures to board a custom-made ark in an orderly manner.

Solved both logistic and staff problems while completing ark under tight deadline. Communicated directly with ark passengers, thus minimizing discord during 40 rough days at sea. Learned how to manage massive enterprise with minimal resources. (1994-Present)

Carpenter, NOAH'S NOTCH
Built structures ranging from book shelves to family houses. Designed ark decks and accommodations for selected clients. (1990-1994)

Education: *School of Hard Knocks*
Bachelor of Biblical Administration
Major: Management

Honors: "Righteous Man in His Generation." Recognized for high moral character and trust of contemporaries.

Leadership
Activities: Chairman, Raven/Dove Contest; Vice President, Ararat 4-H Society

Cover Letter Structure

Let's take a look at the structure of a good cover letter. I recommend four paragraphs:

First Paragraph: Identify your purpose for writing. If someone known to the reader suggested you write, state that fact clearly in the first sentence.

Indicate how you became interested in the particular field or the specific position.

Refer to your educational accomplishments (e.g., MBA, undergraduate biology major) if this is a selling point.

Succinctly refer to past work experience which may be helpful in doing the job for which you are applying.

Second Paragraph: Indicate the benefits and qualifications you offer the employer. Cite specific examples of your accomplishments. Remember—you should not simply repeat the information on your resume. Often, this means emphasizing what is most important *to a specific opportunity* or giving a relevant example of your skills and characteristics.

Third Paragraph: State why you are interested in the *specific job* or type of job. Cite reasons why you want to work for *that specific company*. If possible indicate some level of interest in the *industry* of which the company is a part. Your statements in this paragraph will indicate that you have a sincere, well considered interest in the position for which you are applying. Be sincere and know what you are talking about.

Fourth Paragraph: Make reference to your resume. Indicate that *you will take the next step* (e.g., you will contact the employer's office the following week to arrange a meeting).

Addressing Your Cover Letter

Cover letters should be addressed to a *specific individual* by name and title. It is usually preferable to send your letter and resume to the individual who will make the hiring decision instead of sending them to the Personnel Office. You may call the company directly and ask for the name and title of the executive in the department in which you want to work. Verify position titles and the correct spelling of the addressee's name.

An exception: If you are a college senior, it is acceptable to contact the Director or Manager of College Relations, if the company has one.

Other Considerations In Writing Cover Letters

1. Each cover letter should be tailored to the specific situation and company. "All purpose" cover letters are easily recognized and rejected by employers.
2. Type your cover letter on high quality paper.
3. Include your *return address* on the letter.
4. Check the letter carefully to make sure there are no typing, spelling or grammatical errors.
5. Be sure to SIGN the cover letter in blue or black ink.

Let's take a look at some more sample letters.

Sample Cover Letter (Outreach—Recent College Graduate)

76 Heritage Drive
South Hadley, MA 01007

February 1, 1998

Mr. Robert Iron
Vice President - Marketing
Nutritious Cereals, Inc.
1234 Walnut Street
Philadelphia, PA 19147

Dear Mr. Iron:

I am interested in joining Nutritious Cereals, Inc. in a market research capacity. My interest in this area has developed in the course of several college research projects. Some of the qualifications I can offer your company are:

A solid knowledge of marketing gained while earning a degree in that field. Applied experiences analyzing data and writing recommendations for both businesses and non-profit organizations.

Excellent communication skills, both written and oral. I have written several work situation reports and have given numerous presentations through Junior Chamber of Commerce speakers bureau.

An ambition to succeed. I worked 25 hours per week while attending college full time.

A long standing avocational interest in cereals. For two years I was an officer of the Yum-Yum Breakfast Club.

A career with ABC Cereals, a company praised by the *Wall Street Journal* as "a shining light in the world of corporate marketing," would be very appealing to me. In addition, I wish to work for a medium sized company since that is an environment I have found conducive to gaining a broad perspective on an entire functional area.

My resume is enclosed. On February 8, I will contact your office to see if a meeting can be arranged at your convenience. Thank you.

Sincerely yours,

Larry Kandola

Larry Kandola
Enclosure

Cover Letter (referred by a mutual acquaintance)

293 Wildflower Drive
Minneapolis, MN 55402

June 12, 1998

Ms. Janice Dagi-Ellis
Vice President, Marketing
Enfield Cosmetics
Enfield, CT 06085

Dear Ms. Dagi-Ellis:

Last week I was in Connecticut and had lunch with a mutual acquaintance, Leslie Aarons of Fabulous Footwear. We were discussing my career progress when Leslie mentioned that you are looking for a good product manager. My ten years of experience in consumer products could make me the person you need.

My resume indicates a number of professional accomplishments. However, a personal meeting with you would better indicate if there is a good match between your needs and my talents.

I am eager to explore possibilities with you and I will call you next week to see what you think our next step should be.

Sincerely,

Rhonda Franklin

Rhonda Franklin

cc: Leslie Aarons

Enclosure

Cover Letter (Read article in the Press)

1803 Revere Drive
Boston, MA 02116

September 1, 1998

Dr. Linda Jerome
Alliance Medical Center
95 Portent Street
Hampshire, MI 48203

Dear Dr. Jerome:

I recently saw your name in the *Daily Hampshire Gazette*. Congratulations on the inauguration of your physicians' practices group.

I am looking for an administrative position in a medical practice where I can contribute my skills and drive. Perhaps Alliance Medical Center could benefit from the enthusiasm and business sense that helped me become a successful community leader and office administrator.

My interest in your new practice is rooted in several factors. First, your practice is committed to a community health philosophy that I deeply admire. Second, I believe that physicians' practice groups will be a growing part of health care. Third, I live in the area and am familiar with the Hampshire County Community.

My resume indicates that I have organizational experience, drive and determination. Meeting me in person will convince you that I can apply those talents to a medical practice. I will can you in a few days so we can arrange a meeting.

Sincerely yours,

Lucia Aspiro

Lucia Aspiro

Enclosure

Responding to a Help Wanted Notice

The first step in responding to a help wanted notice is to make a chart. The first two columns match your skills and attributes to the criteria indicated in the notice. This part of the chart will guide you in writing the *second* paragraph of your cover letter. Second, have a separate column to note what motivated you to be interested in this job. This column will help with your *third* paragraph. Third, add a column for identifying any potential objections you may need to overcome.

Let's take a look at a help wanted notice which attracted Beth Golden's attention and see how she wrote an appropriate cover letter in response to it. (Beth's resume is on page 148)

HELP WANTED
MARCH 14, 1998
Submerged Search Corp

Our rapidly growing, hi-tech firm seeks a sea hunt engineer to train an expanding list of clients seeking last fortunes in sunken treasure ships. Client skills, computer competence and a knowledge of the sea a must. Creativity a major plus. Constant relocation on short notice is part of the job.

Respond to: Charles Nemo
               Submerged Search Corp.
               1735 Buccaneer Terrace
               Delray Beach, Florida 33445

Matching Talent of Beth Golden to Criteria of the Notice

Some possible points for Beth to highlight in her cover letter include:

Second Paragraph		Third Paragraph	Possible Objections to overcome
They need	I offer	Motivation is love of sea	Relocation (Note relocations in work history)
Training	Train Crews		
Client Skills	Serve Clients at Laser and Computer Wizard		
Computer Competence	Languages and LAN experience		Not an engineer (Beth decided not to draw attention to this fact in her letter)
Deep Sea	Navy		
Creative	Patents		

96 Holten Road
Bismarck, North Dakota

March 15, 1998

Mr. Charles Nemo
Submerged Search Corp.
1735 Buccaneer Terrace
Delray Beach, Florida 33445

Dear Mr. Nemo:

This is written in response to your notice in the March 14 edition of the *Florida Post* that you are seeking a Sea Hunt Engineer. I am certain that my computer and deep sea experience would make me an asset to your firm. My qualifications for this position include:

Training	Trained people in technical skills since 1996.
Client skills	Worked with both large and small business clients for the last five years.
Computer Competence	Experience with high-end computers and LAN; Expert in JAVA, Scimpy, HTML, C++.
Deep Sea	Petty Officer, Second Class, US Navy with specialized training in Submarine Search, Acoustic Fundamentals and other deep sea search skills.
Creativity	Awarded two patents for novel machine designs.

A position with Submerged Search Corp. would be very appealing to me. My love for the sea and sea hunts developed during my four years of US Navy service. I have remained current in the field by reading *SeaHunt* magazine and by attending unclassified seminars sponsored by the Navy. I am used to frequent relocation from my Navy days and I have relocated twice as a civilian.

My resume is enclosed. I am eager to pursue this career possibility with Submerged Search Corp. Next week, I will contact your office to see what the next step should be.

Sincerely,

Beth Golden

Beth Golden

Enclosure

Index

The Author

R ichard Fein is the Director of Placement at the University of Massachusetts (Amherst) School of Management. A career specialist for 18 years, he is widely recognized as a leading authority on developing the core career planning and job search skills—writing effective resumes and cover letters and conducting winning job interviews. He is author of five major career books on these subjects: ***101 Dynamite Questions to Ask at Your Job Interview***; ***101 Quick Tips For a Dynamite Resume***; ***111 Dynamite Ways to Ace Your Job Interview***; ***Cover Letters! Cover Letter! Cover Letters!*** and ***First Job***.

Richard has been a contributor to the Wall Street Journal's *Managing Your Career* and a columnist for *Employment Review Magazine*. He is a frequent commentator on the job search process for both print and electronic media. He has appeared as a guest on more than 30 radio and television programs and has been quoted in newspapers as diverse as the *Christian Science Monitor* and the *Idaho Statesman*.

Richard holds an MBA from Baruch College in New York, an MA in Political Science from the City University of New York, and a BA in Political Science from the University of Pennsylvania. He can be contacted through Impact Publications or the University of Massachusetts (e-mail: *rfein@som.umass.edu*).

Career Resources

C ontact Impact Publications for a free annotated listing of career resources or visit their World Wide Web site for a complete listing of career resources: *http://www.impactpublications.com*.
The following career resources, many of which were mentioned in previous chapters, are available directly from Impact Publications. Complete the following form or list the titles, include postage (see formula at the end), enclose payment, and send your order to:

IMPACT PUBLICATIONS
9104-N Manassas Drive
Manassas Park, VA 20111-5211
1-800-361-1055 (orders only)
Tel. 703/361-7300 or Fax 703/335-9486
E-mail address: *impactp@impactpublications.com*

Orders from individuals must be prepaid by check, moneyorder, Visa, MasterCard, or American Express. We accept telephone and fax orders.

Qty.	TITLES	Price	TOTAL
Job Search Strategies and Tactics			
___	Change Your Job, Change Your Life	17.95	___
___	Complete Idiot's Guide to Getting the Job You Want	24.95	___
___	Complete Job Finder's Guide to the 90's	13.95	___
___	Five Secrets to Finding a Job	12.95	___
___	How to Get Interviews From Classified Job Ads	14.95	___
___	How to Succeed Without a Career Path	13.95	___
___	Me, Myself, and I, Inc	17.95	___
___	New Rites of Passage at $100,000+	29.95	___

___	The Pathfinder	14.00 ___
___	What Color Is Your Parachute?	16.95 ___

Best Jobs and Employers For the 21st Century

___	50 Coolest Jobs in Sports	15.95 ___
___	Adams Jobs Almanac 1998	15.95 ___
___	American Almanac of Jobs and Salaries	20.00 ___
___	Best Jobs For the 21st Century	19.95 ___
___	Breaking and Entering: Jobs in Film Production	17.95 ___
___	Great Jobs Ahead	11.95 ___
___	Jobs 1998	15.00 ___
___	The Top 100	19.95 ___

Key Directories

___	American Salaries and Wages Survey	110.00 ___
___	Business Phone Book USA 1998	148.00 ___
___	Careers Encyclopedia	39.95 ___
___	Complete Guide to Occupational Exploration	39.95 ___
___	Consultants & Consulting Organizations Directory	565.00 ___
___	Dictionary of Occupational Titles	47.95 ___
___	Encyclopedia of American Industries 1998	520.00 ___
___	Encyclopedia of Associations 1998 (National only)	470.00 ___
___	Encyclopedia of Careers & Vocational Guidance	149.95 ___
___	Enhanced Guide For Occupational Exploration	34.95 ___
___	Enhanced Occupational Outlook Handbook	34.95 ___
___	Hoover's Hot 250	29.95 ___
___	Job Hunter's Sourcebook	70.00 ___
___	National Job Bank 1999	320.00 ___
___	National Trade & Professional Associations 1998	129.00 ___
___	Occupational Outlook Handbook, 1998-99	22.95 ___
___	O*NET Dictionary of Occupational Titles	49.95 ___
___	Professional Careers Sourcebook	99.00 ___
___	Specialty Occupational Outlook: Professions	49.95 ___
___	Specialty Occupational Outlook: Trade & Technical	49.95 ___
___	Vocational Careers Sourcebook	82.00 ___

Education Directories

___	Free and Inexpensive Career Materials	19.95 ___
___	Internships 1999	24.95 ___
___	Peterson's Guide to Graduate & Professional Programs	239.95 ___
___	Peterson's Two- and Four-Year Colleges 1998	45.95 ___
___	Scholarships, Fellowships, & Loans 1998	161.00 ___

Electronic Job Search

___	CareerXroads 1998	22.95 ___
___	Guide to Internet Job Search	14.95 ___
___	How to Get Your Dream Job Using the Web	29.99 ___

Best Companies

___	Hidden Job Market 1999	18.95 ___
___	Hoover's Top 2,500 Employers	22.95 ___

___	Job Vault	20.00 ___
___	JobBank Guide to Computer & High-Tech Companies	16.95 ___
___	JobBank Guide to Health Care Companies	16.95 ___

$100,000+ Jobs

___	The $100,000 Club	25.00 ___
___	100 Winning Resumes For $100,000+ Jobs	24.95 ___
___	201 Winning Cover Letters For $100,000+ Jobs	24.95 ___
___	1500+ KeyWords For $100,000+ Jobs	14.95 ___
___	New Rites of Passage at $100,000+	29.95 ___
___	Six-Figure Consulting	17.95 ___

Finding Great Jobs

___	100 Best Careers in Casinos and Casino Hotels	15.95 ___
___	101 Ways to Power Up Your Job Search	12.95 ___
___	110 Biggest Mistakes Job Hunters Make	19.95 ___
___	Alternative Careers in Secret Operations	19.95 ___
___	Back Door Guide to Short-Term Job Adventures	19.95 ___
___	Careers For College Majors	32.95 ___
___	College Grad Job Hunter	14.95 ___
___	Directory of Executive Recruiters 1998	44.95 ___
___	Get Ahead! Stay Ahead!	12.95 ___
___	Get a Job You Love!	19.95 ___
___	Get What You Deserve!	23.00 ___
___	Great Jobs For Liberal Arts Majors	11.95 ___
___	How to Get Interviews From Classified Job Ads	14.95 ___
___	In Transition	12.50 ___
___	Job Hunting Made Easy	12.95 ___
___	Job Search 101	12.95 ___
___	Jobs & Careers With Nonprofit Organizations	15.95 ___
___	Knock 'Em Dead	12.95 ___
___	New Relocating Spouse's Guide to Employment	14.95 ___
___	No One Is Unemployable	29.95 ___
___	Non-Profits and Education Job Finder	16.95 ___
___	Perfect Pitch	13.99 ___
___	Professional's Job Finder	18.95 ___
___	Strategic Job Jumping	20.00 ___
___	Top Career Strategies For the Year 2000 & Beyond	12.00 ___
___	What Do I Say Next?	20.00 ___
___	What Employers Really Want.	14.95 ___
___	Work Happy Live Healthy	14.95 ___
___	You Can't Play the Game If You Don't Know the Rules	14.95 ___

Assessment

___	Discover the Best Jobs For You	14.95 ___
___	Discover What You're Best At	12.00 ___
___	Do What You Are	16.95 ___
___	Finding Your Perfect Work	16.95 ___
___	I Could Do Anything If Only I Knew What It Was	19.95 ___

Inspiration & Empowerment

___	100 Ways to Motivate Yourself	15.99 ___
___	Chicken Soup For the Soul Series	75.95 ___

___	Doing Work You Love	14.95	___
___	Emotional Intelligence	13.95	___
___	Personal Job Power	12.95	___
___	Power of Purpose	20.00	___
___	Seven Habits of Highly Effective People	14.00	___
___	Survival Personality	12.00	___
___	Your Signature Path	24.95	___

Resumes

___	100 Winning Resumes For $100,000+ Jobs	24.95	___
___	101 Best Resumes	10.95	___
___	101 Quick Tips For a Dynamite Resume	13.95	___
___	1500+ KeyWords For $100,000+ Jobs	14.95	___
___	Adams Resumes Almanac & Disk	19.95	___
___	America's Top Resumes For America's Top Jobs	19.95	___
___	Asher's Bible of Executive Resumes	29.95	___
___	Better Resumes in Three Easy Steps	12.95	___
___	Complete Idiot's Guide to Writing the Perfect Resume	16.95	___
___	Designing the Perfect Resume	12.95	___
___	Dynamite Resumes	14.95	___
___	Encyclopedia of Job-Winning Resumes	16.95	___
___	Gallery of Best Resumes	16.95	___
___	Heart and Soul Resumes	15.95	___
___	High Impact Resumes & Letters	19.95	___
___	Internet Resumes	14.95	___
___	New 90-Minute Resumes	15.95	___
___	New Perfect Resume	12.00	___
___	Portfolio Power	14.95	___
___	Ready-to-Go Resumes	29.95	___
___	Resume Catalog	15.95	___
___	Resume Shortcuts	14.95	___
___	Resumes & Job Search Letters For Transitioning Military Personnel	17.95	___
___	Resumes For Dummies	12.99	___
___	Resumes For Re-Entry	10.95	___
___	Resumes in Cyberspace	14.95	___
___	Resumes That Knock 'Em Dead	14.95	___
___	Sure-Hire Resumes	14.95	___

Cover Letters

___	175 High-Impact Cover Letters	10.95	___
___	201 Dynamite Job Search Letters	19.95	___
___	201 Killer Cover Letters	16.95	___
___	201 Winning Cover Letters For $100,000+ Jobs	24.95	___
___	Adams Cover Letter Almanac & Disk	19.95	___
___	Complete Idiot's Guide to the Perfect Cover Letter	14.95	___
___	Cover Letters For Dummies	12.99	___
___	Cover Letters That Knock 'Em Dead	10.95	___
___	Dynamite Cover Letters	14.95	___

Networking

___	Dynamite Networking For Dynamite Jobs	15.95	___
___	Dynamite Telesearch	12.95	___
___	Great Connections	19.95	___
___	How to Work a Room	11.99	___

___ People Power	14.95	___
___ Power Networking	14.95	___
___ Power Schmoozing	12.95	___
___ Power to Get In	24.95	___

Interview & Communication Skills

___ 90-Minute Interview Prep Book	15.95	___
___ 101 Dynamite Answers to Interview Questions	12.95	___
___ 101 Dynamite Questions to Ask At Your Job Interview	14.95	___
___ 101 Great Answers to the Toughest Interview Questions	9.99	___
___ 101 Secrets of Highly Effective Speakers	14.95	___
___ 111 Dynamite Ways to Ace Your Job Interview	13.95	___
___ Complete Idiot's Guide to the Perfect Job Interview	14.95	___
___ Complete Q & A Job Interview Book	14.95	___
___ Interview For Success	15.95	___
___ Interview Power	12.95	___
___ Job Interview For Dummies	12.99	___

Salary Negotiations

___ Dynamite Salary Negotiations	15.95	___
___ Get More Money On Your Next Job	14.95	___
___ Negotiate Your Job Offer	14.95	___

SUBTOTAL ___

Virginia residents add 4½% sales tax ___

POSTAGE/HANDLING ($5 for first
product and 8% of SUBTOTAL over $30) $5.00

8% of SUBTOTAL over $30 -------------------------- ___

TOTAL ENCLOSED ------------------------- ___

NAME _____

ADDRESS _____

_____

_____

❑ I enclose check/moneyorder for $ _____ made payable to
     IMPACT PUBLICATIONS.

❑ Please charge $ _____ to my credit card:
     ❑ Visa   ❑ MasterCard   ❑ American Express   ❑ Discover

     Card # _____

     Expiration date: _____/_____

     Signature _____

The On-Line Superstore & Warehouse

Hundreds of Terrific Career Resources Conveniently Available On the World Wide Web 24-Hours a Day, 365 Days a Year!

Ever wanted to know what are the newest and best books, directories, newsletters, wall charts, training programs, videos, CD-ROMs, computer software, and kits available to help you land a job, negotiate a higher salary, or start your own business? What about finding a job in Asia or relocating to San Francisco? Are you curious about how to find a job 24-hours a day by using the Internet or what you'll be doing five years from now? Trying to keep up-to-date on the latest career resources but not able to find the latest catalogs, brochures, or newsletters on today's "best of the best" resources?

Welcome to the first virtual career bookstore on the Internet. Now you're only a "click" away with Impact Publication's electronic solution to the resource challenge. Impact Publications, one of the nation's leading publishers and distributors of career resources, has launched its comprehensive "Career Superstore and Warehouse" on the Internet. The bookstore is jam-packed with the latest job and career resources on:

- Alternative jobs and careers
- Self-assessment
- Career planning and job search
- Employers
- Relocation and cities
- Resumes
- Cover Letters
- Dress, image, and etiquette
- Education
- Telephone
- Military
- Salaries
- Interviewing
- Nonprofits
- Empowerment
- Self-esteem
- Goal setting
- Executive recruiters
- Entrepreneurship
- Government
- Networking
- Electronic job search
- International jobs
- Travel
- Law
- Training and presentations
- Minorities
- Physically challenged

The bookstore also includes a new "Military Career Transition Center" and "School-to-Work Center."

"This is more than just a bookstore offering lots of product," say Drs. Ron and Caryl Krannich, two of the nation's leading career experts and authors and developers of this on-line bookstore. *"We're an important resource center for libraries, corporations, government, educators, trainers, and career counselors who are constantly defining and redefining this dynamic field. Of the thousands of career resources we review each year, we only select the 'best of the best.'"*

Visit this rich site and you'll quickly discover just about everything you ever wanted to know about finding jobs, changing careers, and starting your own business—including many useful resources that are difficult to find in local bookstores and libraries. The site also includes what's new and hot, tips for job search success, and monthly specials. Impact's Web address is:

http://www.impactpublications.com